BEST
Dental
MARKETING

HOW TO LEVERAGE AI, VIDEO, SOCIAL MEDIA,
AND MORE FOR NEW PATIENT GROWTH

VERSION 1

BRAD NEWMAN

FOUNDER + CHIEF BUZZ OFFICER @DENTAINMENT

Copyright 2023 © by Dentainment

All rights reserved. No part of this book may be used or reproduced in any manner whatsoever without written permission except in the case of brief quotations embodied in critical articles or reviews.

Thank you for purchasing an authorized edition of this book and for complying with copyright laws by not reproducing, scanning, or distributing any part of it in any form without permission. By doing so, you are supporting writers and their hard work.

Published in the United States of America

First Printing Edition, 2023

ISBN: 9798850521172

FOR OUR AMAZING CLIENTS, WHO ALLOW US TO DO WHAT WE LOVE!

TABLE OF CONTENTS

Chapter 1:	One Minute Of Video Is Worth 1.8 Million Words	17
Chapter 2:	The Power of the Play Button	19
Chapter 3:	Debunking Myths and Overcoming Obstacles - Embracing Video Marketing	22
Chapter 4:	Overcoming Barriers and Harnessing Opportunities - Creating Impactful Videos	25
Chapter 5:	No-Camera Strategies From Patient Testimonials to Animated Videos	28
Chapter 6:	Video Social Proof for Success and Beyond	31
Chapter 7:	Starting Strong - Initial Considerations For Crafting Your Video Marketing Strategy	33
Chapter 8:	Storyboarding For Success	36
Chapter 9:	The Art Of Video Marketing For Cosmetic Dentistry And Implant Dentistry	40
Chapter 10:	Break the Stage Fright to Speak Confidently On Camera	43
Chapter 11:	Harnessing Video Marketing to Amplify Your Online Persona and Foster Profound Relationships with Your Patients	46
Chapter 12:	That's a Wrap - Creating a High-Powered Post-Filming Dental Marketing Strategy	55
Chapter 13:	Dental Websites - Mastering Conversion Rate Optimization for New Patient Growth	57

Chapter 14:	Keyword Optimization - Uplifting User Experience and Online Success	67
Chapter 15:	Embracing Voice-Based Apps for CRO and Brand Visibility	72
Chapter 16:	Mastering Local SEO and Maximizing Your Google Presence	75
Chapter 17:	PPC for Dental Marketing ROI - A Word About Google AdWords	81
Chapter 18:	Social Media for Dentists - What Should We Post?	85
Chapter 19:	Harnessing the Power of Dental Content - Fostering Strong Bonds with Teams and Patients	91
Chapter 20:	Infusing Humor and Humanity in Your Dental Marketing Content	96
Chapter 21:	Revolutionizing Dental Practice Marketing with Artificial Intelligence - Key Principles and Effective Strategies	103
Chapter 22:	Unleashing the Power of ChatGPT in Dental Marketing - Insights, Examples, and Success Stories	109
Chapter 23:	Harnessing the Power of Reviews for Dental Practice Success - A Deep Dive into Strategies, Impact, and Best Practices	113
Chapter 24:	Navigating the Crossroads of Traditional and Digital Marketing to Ensure Dental Practice Success	116
Chapter 25:	Leveraging the Power of Dual Marketing - Traditional and Digital Marketing Strategies Practice Growth	119
Chapter 26:	Harnessing the Potential of Print Media and Deep Media Nurturing	123
Chapter 27:	Unleashing the Potential of Your Dental Team - The Art of Empowerment	126

Chapter 28:	Cultivating Your Dental Brand - The Essence of Authenticity	130
Chapter 29:	Crafting the Ideal Logo - Articulating Your Dental Brand	133
Chapter 30:	Elevating Your Dental Practice Through Strategic Design	139
Chapter 31:	Mastering the Art of Branding Your Dental Practice	143
Chapter 32:	Is Your Dental Practice Instagrammable?	146
Chapter 33:	Harnessing The Power Of Threads In Dental Marketing	148
Chapter 34:	A Deeper Dive into Dental Memberships - Unleashing Potential and Expanding Patient Care	151
Chapter 35:	Amplifying Your Dental Practice through Referral Marketing	154
Chapter 36:	Setting Your Marketing Goals and Objectives	158
Chapter 37:	Navigating the Return on Investment in Your Dental Marketing Plan	161
Chapter 38:	Augmented Reality - Revolutionizing Dental Marketing	164
Chapter 39:	Destination Dental Visitors - Attracting Out-Of-Town Patients	167
Chapter 40:	Implementing In-Office Seminars to Stand-Out and Attract New Patients	169
Chapter 41:	Your Next Steps - Mastering the Art of Dental Marketing	172
Dental Marketing Plan Worksheets		180
Our Best Dental Marketing Ideas Journal Area		186

Hi esteemed Dentist or Dental Team member,

Firstly, a heartfelt THANK YOU for choosing this book! It's our sincere hope that the pages within will inspire you not only to infuse more fun into your Dental Marketing efforts, but also to get your creative juices flowing with engaging daily content, and ultimately, to realize tremendous success in attracting high-quality new patients.

That said, we recognize the unique nature of every Dental Practice. Each practice possesses its unique focus on specific services, a distinct demographic of targeted patients, different levels of local competition, and a unique timeline of operation. Given these complexities and nuances, it's likely that each reader will bring their own set of needs and interests to this book. Consequently, we encourage you to navigate this book in whatever order you see fit. While the book is packed with a plethora of groundbreaking recommendations, the successful implementation of even just ONE can catapult your Practice to an entirely new level of success.

Furthermore, as we delve into the world of Digital Marketing, we must acknowledge the burgeoning impact of artificial intelligence (AI). Tools like OpenAI's ChatGPT are revolutionizing the way we approach online engagement. These powerful AI models can be deployed to manage patient inquiries, schedule appointments, or provide automated responses on social media, among other tasks. Embracing such technology can provide a cutting-edge to your Practice's online presence.

In the development of this book, we encountered numerous iterations and self-imposed delays. This was primarily due to the rapid changes in the Digital Marketing landscape. Campaign Strategies for offices and presentations need frequent updates and revisions. We're witnessing an upward trend in platforms like TikTok (until the inevitable ban), while organic reach on Facebook seems to be making a strong comeback. These trends shift constantly. Given this, we urge you to focus more on the broader messages of this book and less on specific platforms. While behemoths like Facebook, Instagram, YouTube, and Google are likely here to stay, the future of many other platforms remains uncertain (i.e. SnapChat).

Therefore, keep a keen eye on the data, stay ahead of emerging trends, and surround yourself with the most competent Dental Marketing Team you can assemble.

Take pleasure in reading this book and continue with your inspiring work!

Should you have any questions, feedback, or simply wish to drop a friendly greeting, don't hesitate to send us an email to info@dentainment.com or visit BestDentalMarketing.com for additional resources from this book.

All the best,

Brad Newman

Founder + Chief Buzz Officer @dentainment

PREFACE

Before we dive into the finer details of this guide, there's an important question that needs to be addressed: why the name "Best Dental Marketing"?

Certainly, there were many potential choices for the book title – dozens of options that could have encapsulated the essence of its content. So, why did "Best Dental Marketing" stick? Here's why:

1. **Trending Search Terms:** Google searches using the term "Best" are growing exponentially, especially in relation to local businesses such as Dental Practices (think "Best Dentist Near Me"). We thought it would be powerful to lean into this trend that's relevant to all topics in this book.

2. **Customization and Impact:** Every Dental Practice is unique and requires a tailored set of initiatives for their desired ROI. The phrase "Best Dental Marketing" represents our top recommendations designed to have the most impact for readers, regardless of their unique situations.

3. **Cutting Through the Noise:** The online landscape is saturated with content. Social Media platforms and search results are flooded with an abundance of information, making it crucial for this book to have a title that can be quickly identified while scrolling through a platform like Amazon.

4. **Memorable Title:** The domain name associated with "Best Dental Marketing" was available and it provides a catchy, easy-to-remember title.

5. **SEO Relevance:** Despite Google's statement that "descriptive domain names" no longer benefit SEO, we believe they do. Throughout this book, we'll delve into some of our contrarian views on rankings, content, and other Digital Marketing strategies that will certainly help your practice's entire digital-footprint.

Built by Dental Marketing Experts

The insights shared in this book were conceived by Brad Newman, a Dental Marketing expert and the Founder and Chief Buzz Officer of Dentainment, along with Team members of this Digital Marketing Agency. Since 2010, the Dentainment Team has been creating immersive marketing experiences for Dental Practices across the United States. For over a decade, our clients have leveraged our agency's expertise to devise high-converting, high-ROI marketing strategies, enabling them to grow their patient base. We've lectured at numerous conferences, showcasing how Dental Practices can leverage the power of our unique strategies. Now, we are sharing these strategies in "Best Dental Marketing", to help Dental Practices everywhere attract new patients, boost revenues, and inspire their Team members to be more involved in marketing initiatives.

INTRODUCTION

Where to begin? Let's kick off with arguably the most potent form of multimedia content one can generate: VIDEO. However, before we delve into that, we need to address something even more critical—ensuring your practice doesn't have an Access to Care issue!

As of this book's writing, an unintentional Access to Care issue stands as the most prominent problem plaguing many practices. In essence, Access to Care refers to how readily available your services are to your patients. It becomes problematic when new patients encounter hurdles booking appointments. Here are some common obstacles:

1. Your online scheduling isn't showing openings for months: If that's the case, how can anyone book an appointment? We've found that having new patient slots available around 8:30 AM and 2:00 PM yields high conversions.

2. Your website's contact form is malfunctioning, and you're unaware: This problem is common with WordPress websites, especially when using Outlook for email. Regular testing of your website contact forms is crucial. Just remember to use fictional patient names and cross-check with your front desk to confirm receipt.

3. Your office phone goes unanswered: It's perplexing how an office could leave phone calls unanswered or neglect to hire a reputable call answering service for after-hours. Data suggests that 35% of people who reach an answering machine never call back. Additionally, only 1 out of 6 calls to an office get answered.

4. Unanswered DM (Direct Messages) on Facebook or Instagram: When potential patients' inquiries go unanswered for a lengthy period, they typically won't attempt to reconnect.

A multitude of factors may contribute to missed opportunities for new patient conversions, often due to broken funnels. Regular checks and repairs of these are vital. Before spending another dollar on marketing or trying any strategy outlined in this book, ensure your new LEADS are captured and responded to promptly.

Always remember: Answer your phone with a smile—it resonates in your voice! Treat every new inquiry like the most significant potential patient for your Dental Practice. Embodying this "availability vibe" and cultivating an open-minded Dental Team can yield incredible opportunities.

"The golden rule for every businessman is this: Put yourself in your customer's place." - Orison Swett Marden.

Now, let's return to the fun part.

CHAPTER 1: ONE MINUTE OF VIDEO IS WORTH 1.8 MILLION WORDS

Indeed, you read that correctly. Have you considered the potential impact of those 1.8 million words on your Dental Practice?

At 30 frames per second, every second of video delivers the impact of 30,000 words. Multiply that by your video's length, and you'll get a sense of your video's worth.

While this might be an anecdote, it underscores the heightened impact of video over still images. Imagine communicating the equivalent of 1.8 million words! Though you're not literally saying that much, you're communicating vastly more through thoughts, emotions, connections, and memories.

This book will explore the power of video marketing in great depth for today's Dental Practices. More than merely discussing its power, we aim to provide actionable insights into incorporating video into your marketing strategies. In this way, you can leverage one of today's most influential marketing channels to share your Dental Practice's story.

We have seen video content's power firsthand with our clients and will be sharing the most impactful aspects of their content initiatives. Our goal is to distill years of marketing insights and lessons into actionable steps for you today.

In this journey, we will delve into how our clients have utilized video content to create lasting impressions and effectively convey their brand's message. We'll explore various facets - from informative videos explaining complex Dental procedures to heartwarming testimonials of satisfied patients. These videos not only humanize the Dental Practice but also serve as a form of reassurance to potential patients, showcasing the technical skill and patient care that sets your practice apart. By translating the practical wisdom gathered over the years into actionable steps, we aim to equip you with the tools necessary to harness the full potential of video marketing in today's digital age.

"Every video you post, every image you feature, every infographic you create, every blog post you write should depict and amplify your core message and brand."

- Rebekah Radice

CHAPTER 2: THE POWER OF THE PLAY BUTTON

"The aim of marketing is to know and understand the customer so well the product or service fits him and sells itself."

~ Peter Drucker

As a Dental Practice owner or Team member, you're part of a world that buzzes incessantly, relentlessly vying for attention. In this context, the landscape of marketing is an intense battleground where companies employ increasingly creative strategies to captivate interest. However, amidst this dynamic, multi-channel marketing noise, the prospect of making a genuine impact might seem overwhelming. But worry not, because the transformative power of video marketing is at your disposal.

Just like all businesses, Dental Practices face these marketing challenges, yet they are armed with a tool that carries a potent punch – the video. The thought of stepping in front of the camera might be nerve-wracking for many Dentists or Dental Team members, but it's essential to view it as an opportunity rather than a hurdle. The questions – What to say? What to wear? What equipment is needed? Where to post videos? – are all part of the process. Through this book, we will explore these questions and more. Remember, videos not only have the power to sell your practice, but they can also imbue it with a personal touch, an authenticity that today's audiences crave and appreciate.

The Magic Of Stories

"Marketing is no longer about the stuff that you make, but about the stories you tell."

~ Seth Godin

Storytelling, a tradition as old as humanity itself, holds a profound place in the human experience. It engages emotions and, as research shows, emotions form the driving force behind purchasing decisions. Mastering the art of storytelling in your Dental Practice opens up a realm of opportunities. It helps attract new patient demographics, strengthens trust with existing patients, positions you as an industry leader, and resonates emotionally with your audience.

Telling Your Story Through Video

In this rapidly evolving marketing world, traditional methods such as sales-type ads or mailings are no longer the most effective marketing strategies. Video storytelling has emerged as a favored approach, bringing your Dental Practice's story to life. A recent HubSpot State of Marketing Report noted video as the top format businesses leverage for marketing their services. Wyzowl's study further corroborates this trend, revealing that 87% of businesses saw increased website traffic, and 80% reported a direct surge in sales due to video marketing.

Videos are concise, memorable, and uniquely equipped to convey complex information. They provide a personal touch, helping patients feel your warmth and sincerity. Patient testimonials through video are particularly effective in building trust, as they prove that your reviews are genuine, coming from real people.

"The amount of information contained in one single frame can take three pages to describe. It is a known fact that people engage more when they watch a video and tend to stay watching it. They are also happy to pass it along. Video informs and entertains people and, good or bad, today most people prefer to watch a video rather than read a page of text."

~ Lisa Lubin

Your Blueprint For Video Success

This book serves as your guide to embracing and mastering video marketing. It will explore various topics, including:

- Topic selection, types of videos, and their purposes.
- Sets, lights, sound, and gear.
- Preparations for filming day, focusing on appearance and live versus recorded videos.
- Strategies on where to post your videos, generating views, and tracking their effectiveness.
- Key statistics about video marketing.
- Resources to streamline your content initiatives.

The ultimate goal of this book is to highlight the significance of video marketing and provide you with actionable strategies that will help you generate new patients, build trust, and elevate your Dental Practice's brand awareness within your community.

If you've read this far, it's clear you understand the value of marketing. Let us help you take your Dental Practice to the next level with practical insights and tips. We're in an era where the play button truly is the most compelling call-to-action on the web. Let's harness its power and step into the future of marketing together.

"Take a risk and keep testing, because what works today won't work tomorrow, but what worked yesterday may work again."

~Amrita Sahasrabudhe

CHAPTER 3: DEBUNKING MYTHS AND OVERCOMING OBSTACLES - EMBRACING VIDEO MARKETING

"Video is an effective form of communication that needs to be integrated into each and every aspect of your existing marketing efforts."

- James Wedmore

Following the exploration of the importance of video marketing in Chapter 1, we will delve deeper into the psychology of why some are hesitant to adopt this powerful tool. If your Dental Practice hasn't yet embraced video marketing, it's crucial to understand the reasons behind this hesitation, as well as strategies for overcoming these obstacles.

The growing prevalence of video is undeniable, and those not utilizing this medium risk falling behind. Therefore, it's essential to question your apprehensions and consider the benefits that await on the other side. With this book, our goal is to provide a roadmap towards confident and effective video marketing. We don't want your Dental Practice to lag behind, and by picking up this book, you've shown you don't want that either.

We will delve into the intricate details of video marketing, from its concept to production and distribution, in upcoming chapters. But before we navigate these waters, it's crucial to address the common objections and psychological barriers that deter individuals from making videos.

Debunking the Misconceptions of Video Marketing

Now, let's have an honest conversation. Many objections that justify avoiding video marketing aren't based on reality. In fact, they can often be comforting lies that shield us from confronting our fears.

Yes, standing in front of a camera can be intimidating, and creating an engaging video marketing campaign requires effort. However, overcoming these initial hesitations and pressing the record button can unlock unprecedented growth for your Dental Practice.

Let's demystify some common "lies" Dental Practice owners tell themselves, providing reasons for why video marketing isn't an option for them.

My Appearance on Camera Is Unflattering

It's okay. You're not alone in this concern. Most people are hypercritical of their appearance on camera. However, we are often our own harshest critics, scrutinizing details others wouldn't notice. Remember, you don't need to present yourself with professional makeup, hairstyling, or expensive attire to feel confident on video. Your expertise and authenticity in your field will always overshadow any superficial judgments.

"You don't have to be great to start, but you have to start to be great."

~ Zig Ziglar

Fear of Public Speaking

The fear of public speaking is one of the most common phobias, affecting a large percentage of the population. This fear can be exacerbated when a camera is involved. But remember, video marketing doesn't have to be live, and it doesn't have to be perfect. Video provides the unique advantage of retakes and edits. Plus, the more you practice, the more comfortable you will become.

Lack of Technical Know-how

While video production can seem daunting, advancements in technology have made the process increasingly user-friendly. Simple, high-quality videos can be filmed using devices most of us carry in our pockets – smartphones. There are countless resources available, including this book, that can guide you through the process step by step.

Your journey towards effective video marketing might feel like a daunting leap right now, but remember, even the longest journey begins with a single step. Let's take that step together and unveil the transformative power of video for your Dental Practice. The play button awaits.

"Action is the foundational key to all success."

~ Pablo Picasso

CHAPTER 4: OVERCOMING BARRIERS AND HARNESSING OPPORTUNITIES - CREATING IMPACTFUL VIDEOS

"The biggest risk is not taking any risk... In a world that's changing really quickly, the only strategy that is guaranteed to fail is not taking risks."

~ Mark Zuckerberg

Having explored some common concerns about venturing into video marketing, this chapter will discuss how you can navigate these potential obstacles. Whether you feel uncomfortable about how you sound on camera, are unsure about your video creation skills, or are daunted by the perceived high cost, it's important to know that you are not alone. These concerns are common, but thankfully, they can be overcome.

The Sound of Your Voice

Many people feel apprehensive about how they sound on camera. If this resonates with you, rest assured, you're not the only one. Preparing a script beforehand can help manage these anxieties. The use of cue cards or a teleprompter app can also assist you in articulating your points. Remember that, just as with appearance, you're often more conscious about your voice than your viewers are.

Lacking Skills in Video Creation

You might worry about lacking the skills necessary to create impressive videos. We will discuss this in more depth in later chapters, but for now, understand that you don't need to be a tech wizard to create engaging videos. Simplicity can be remarkably effective in Dental videos. You may find that there are members of your Dental Team who possess the skills you're lacking and are willing to help. If your budget allows, hiring a professional production company could also be an option. Moreover, the tools and resources available today enable even those with a modest budget to create high-quality videos.

Inadequate Tools for Video Creation

With the internet at your disposal, finding resources for video creation is as simple as typing a search query. From free services to those requiring minimal monthly fees, there's no shortage of available tools. Thanks to the advancement of smartphone technology, expensive video cameras and lighting equipment aren't necessary, though they remain an option if you prefer not to use your phone. The rise of mobile technology has even led to film festivals accepting submissions shot exclusively on smartphones!

"The way to get started is to quit talking and begin doing."

~ Walt Disney

Concern About High Costs

The perception of video marketing as an expensive venture is a common misconception. The reality is that many Dental Practices allocate a reasonably small fraction of their marketing budgets to video creation. With the utilization of free or low-cost tools, and capitalizing on your team's skills, video creation doesn't have to strain your budget. Furthermore, the ability to repurpose video content further enhances its value, resulting in a return on investment that surpasses other forms of content.

Not Knowing Where to Start

Like any new venture, you won't be an expert in video marketing right away, but with time and experience, you'll improve. We'll discuss video topics and content later in this book. Remember, today's audiences appreciate authenticity and value-driven content. Initiating your video marketing journey by simply hitting record and sharing insights about your Dental Practice can be a great start. Often, less polished videos, thanks to their authenticity, can outperform highly produced ones.

Strategies for the Camera-Shy

Even if you've read through these common concerns and still feel uneasy about appearing on camera, that doesn't exclude you from using video marketing. While you might be camera-shy, others around you may be more comfortable on camera. Utilizing these individuals can greatly enhance your video marketing campaign and extend your Dental Practice's reach.

Self-awareness is important. If you feel you'd rather not appear in front of the camera, find those who are willing, or consider creative alternatives. Remember, one of the strengths of video is its ability to show, not just tell. From tutorials and animations to point-of-view experiences, there's a plethora of ways to create impactful videos without personally appearing on camera.

In the next sections, we'll explore how you can continue to incorporate video into your marketing strategy, even without putting yourself in the spotlight. The possibilities are exciting and endless, ready for you to seize and adapt to your Dental Practice. Remember, progress is better than perfection, and every step you take towards video marketing is a step towards growth.

"Film provides an opportunity to marry the power of ideas with the power of images."

~ Steven Bochco

CHAPTER 5: NO-CAMERA STRATEGIES FROM PATIENT TESTIMONIALS TO ANIMATED VIDEOS

"Good content isn't about good storytelling. It's about telling a true story well."

~ Ann Handley

In this chapter, we will explore various ways to utilize video marketing strategies without requiring your direct presence on camera. You'll discover that there are numerous alternatives to traditional video production that can still effectively engage your audience and tell your Dental Practice's story.

Patient Testimonials: The Power of Social Proof

One of the most effective selling strategies is social proof. Inviting patients to share their positive experiences on camera can not only help establish social proof, but also further humanize your Dental Practice. You can maintain a behind-the-camera role while letting your patients take center stage. When executed well, video testimonials can be an influential form of social proof and an incredible marketing tool.

Screen-Share Videos: Walkthroughs and Tutorials

Screen-share videos can offer a clear, step-by-step demonstration of how certain processes work. Whether you're guiding patients through your online booking system or showcasing the capabilities of CEREC Same Day Crowns, a screen-share video with a friendly voice-over (yours or a team member's) can effectively communicate your points. Tools like Camtasia make recording these types of videos straightforward and easy.

Slideshows: A Wealth of Information

Slideshows can serve as an educational tool for your audience, covering various aspects of oral health or your Dental Practice's operations. With the aid of readily available presentation software like PowerPoint, Keynote, Prezi, or Canva, you can record your screen and voice simultaneously to deliver valuable information to your patients. Topics like TMJ or Dental Sleep Apnea are excellent subjects for slideshow presentations. Additionally, these presentations can be transformed into evergreen webinars, remaining accessible on your website indefinitely.

Point-Of-View Videos: A Unique Perspective

By investing in a GoPro or similar camera technology, you can record point-of-view videos that provide a unique perspective. Whether it's a virtual tour of your office or a first-hand perspective of a Dental procedure, these videos can create an engaging experience without requiring you to appear on camera.

Service Videos: Detailed Explanations

Every service your Dental Practice provides could have a corresponding video embedded on your website. Your website itself can serve as a script to create videos for each of your services, from Invisalign and Cosmetic Dentistry to Dental Cleanings and Exams.

Animated Videos: Engaging and Fun

Animated videos can create an engaging experience without requiring anyone to appear on camera. While they may require more planning and potentially additional costs, animated videos can cover virtually any Dental-related topic, making them a flexible tool for your marketing needs.

Kinetic Typography: Words in Motion

Kinetic typography videos use animated text to convey your message, often accompanied by background music to maintain audience engagement. These videos can perform exceptionally well on social media and compliment live-action videos.

Stock Footage: A Ready-Made Solution

If you're uncertain where to start, stock footage can be a valuable resource. With a wide range of industries and purposes covered, you can purchase stock footage and then customize it with text overlays, voice-overs, or music to suit your Dental Practice. Remember to ensure you have the appropriate usage rights for any stock footage you use.

In the chapters to come, we'll delve into the practical aspects of implementing these strategies into your video marketing campaign. As you'll discover, each strategy presents unique advantages that can effectively engage your audience, promote your Dental Practice, and grow your patient base.

CHAPTER 6: VIDEO SOCIAL PROOF FOR SUCCESS AND BEYOND

"Marketing is telling the world you're a rock star. Content Marketing is showing the world you are one."

~ Robert Rose

As we delve deeper into the world of video marketing, this chapter provides bonus insights into crafting powerful video testimonials. Implementing these tips can significantly enhance your testimonials' impact, turning them into compelling marketing assets for your Dental Practice.

10 Tips for Capturing Powerful Video Testimonials

1. **Crafting a Starting Sentence:** Begin by asking your patients, "What do you like most about our Dental Office?" This question can provide a launchpad for their testimonial.
2. **Life-Changing Impact:** Ask, "Did your treatment change your life?" This question can elicit powerful, personal stories about the value of your services.
3. **Filming Location:** Opt for filming in an operatory or another Dental setting. This choice helps signal the content's relevance from the thumbnail itself.
4. **Showcasing Smiles:** Encourage patients to smile and show off their pearly whites. After all, a healthy, happy smile is the best advertisement for a Dental Practice.
5. **Adding Movement:** Begin the video with a wave or a smile, indicating to viewers that it's a video, not a static image.

6. **Setting Expectations:** Start conversations about these video ideas with patients during prior appointments.

7. **Device Selection:** Use your own device (preferably a mobile phone) to capture these testimonials. This approach can often make the process seem less intimidating to the patient.

8. **Multiple Takes:** Don't hesitate to do more than one take. The patient might need a few tries to warm up and include all crucial points in their testimonial.

9. **Patient Release Forms:** Always ensure you have a signed patient release form for video testimonials, safeguarding both parties' rights and interests.

10. **Systematizing the Process:** Establish a system for sending the files for proper optimization and uploading to your chosen platforms.

Final Thoughts: Overcoming Camera Shyness

Video remains an indispensable tool for any Dental Practice's marketing strategy. Despite self-proclaimed camera shyness, there are countless ways to integrate video marketing into your Practice. We've explored several strategies that can help you use video effectively without having to be the primary on-camera personality. If you're not comfortable in front of the camera, remember that you might have team members or patients who are. Leveraging their enthusiasm and skills can help make video marketing a reality, boosting your Dental Practice's exposure, and expanding your reach to a broader audience of prospective patients.

"Clickthroughs on a video are often much higher than a standard website listing on the front page of Google. If you see a video in the Google results… it stands out a lot more than a regular website listing does, so it tends to attract more clicks."

~ Matt Carter

CHAPTER 7: STARTING STRONG - INITIAL CONSIDERATIONS FOR CRAFTING YOUR VIDEO MARKETING STRATEGY

"Traditional marketing talks at people. Content marketing talks with them."

~ Doug Kessler

Video marketing is revolutionizing how businesses communicate with their audiences, and Dental Practices are no exception. In this chapter, we delve into the purpose of video marketing, how to get started with topic selection, and the types of videos to consider. Here, we aim to orient you to the WHY, WHAT, and HOW of video marketing.

Understanding Video Marketing

If a picture is worth a thousand words, a video is worth millions. Video marketing is the strategy of promoting your business and narrating your Dental Practice's story through various types of video content. It can significantly increase engagement on your Dental website, social media channels, and educate your audience, allowing you to reach existing and new patients in a refreshing medium. The key to effective video marketing, however, is strategic planning.

The Importance of Video Marketing

Video consumption is continuously increasing, and it's what your audience wants. Reports suggest that a significant majority of consumers rely on videos to understand products or services, and many make purchasing decisions based on them. Moreover, businesses worldwide recognize the value of video marketing and incorporate it into their strategies. If you're not already using video as a marketing strategy for your Dental Practice, it's time to get started.

Overcoming Video Marketing Objections

Stepping out from behind the Dental chair and standing in front of the camera can be daunting. There are numerous reasons why brands avoid video marketing, ranging from a lack of time and understanding to concerns about cost and ROI. However, today's audiences crave authenticity and a quick live video recorded on your phone can drive brand engagement effectively and inexpensively.

Identifying Your "Why"

"Working hard for something we don't care about is called stress; working hard for something we love is called passion."

- Simon Sinek

Before embarking on a video marketing journey, it's vital to understand your purpose for doing so. Are you looking to engage current patients, attract new ones, or establish yourself as a thought leader in the Dental industry? Sketching out your motivations and desired outcomes will guide your video strategies, content, and overall success.

Types of Dental Videos to Consider

Once you've committed to incorporating video into your marketing strategy, it's important to familiarize yourself with the various types of videos used in marketing. The choice of video type should be based on your objectives, budget, and the preferences of your target audience.

Crowdsource ideas from your Dental Team and encourage discussions on the kind of content that could be created.

Choosing Your Topics Wisely

Regardless of the video type, the content is king. A good rule of thumb is to start with topics and ideas that will deliver the most significant ROI for your Dental Practice. Brainstorming ideas with your Dental Team can yield powerful content that brings value to your audience.

In the world of marketing, teamwork indeed makes the dream work. As you embark on your video marketing journey, remember to listen, learn, and leverage the unique insights of your team. With careful planning, strategic execution, and a little creativity, your Dental practice can truly shine in the world of video marketing.

"In the same way that each frame contributes to a complete video, every team member contributes to the final project."

CHAPTER 8: STORYBOARDING FOR SUCCESS

"Storyboarding in Dental marketing is like a Dentist planning a treatment. Each scene is carefully crafted, like each tooth is meticulously treated, to form a perfect smile on the face of the audience."

The art of creating engaging and successful videos commences long before the camera starts rolling. It starts with a simple yet powerful tool: a storyboard. Storyboarding is a crucial aspect of video creation, helping you visualize your narrative and plan for any potential hitches. Whether you draw it out on pieces of paper, use PowerPoint with stock images, or opt for professional storyboarding software, it all boils down to putting your ideas into a visual form.

A well-designed storyboard is a roadmap for your video. It allows you to see the bigger picture without overlooking the minute details. This systematic approach provides a clear direction and helps you foresee any potential obstacles that may interrupt the smooth flow of your narrative. Notably, it allows you to make changes and fine-tune your story more efficiently, making your video more coherent and engaging.

Just as a compelling marketing story, a good storyboard should have key elements that serve to hold your audience's attention and guide them through your narrative. These include an appealing hook, the demonstration of a problem that resonates with the viewers, a compelling presentation of the solution, addressing potential doubts or objections, and finally, a convincing call-to-action. These elements help ensure your video is not just entertaining, but also persuasive and effective in achieving its purpose.

As you brainstorm topics for your video, shift your mindset from sales to storytelling. This shift is crucial because, in essence, your audience wants to be captivated by stories, not sold to. In this regard, your marketing videos can span a wide array of topics, so don't be afraid to get creative.

You could produce educational how-to videos leveraging your expertise in Dental Health. Try shooting fun videos to help relax patients in the waiting room. Engage your audience with Dental Q & A sessions or demonstration videos, which can be shared on platforms like YouTube and social media. You could also consider co-hosting a Dental program with a colleague or hosting a call-in podcast, allowing guests to interact with you directly.

Additionally, you can capitalize on popular topics related to your specialty to attract more viewers. For instance, if you specialize in Cosmetic Dentistry, create videos that mirror your specialty. Don't forget to keep your patients informed about the latest advancements and services in your practice. A fun Q & A session with your Dental Team or social media polls can also serve to engage your audience and give you ideas for future video topics.

As you create your video, remember to capture your audience's attention within the first few seconds. People's attention spans are short, and a long-winded intro can easily deter them from watching the rest of your video. Consider long-form videos as well. While they require more time and effort, they can foster deeper emotional connections with your audience.

Creating a series of videos that provides a glimpse into your Dental Practice, such as "a day in the life of," can offer a unique perspective and build a stronger bond with your audience. Videos that showcase your team and your work environment can make your practice seem more approachable and friendly. Alternatively, you might want to consider an ongoing web series or podcasts, which have gained popularity in recent years.

Here's an example storyboard on Dental Implants for inspiration:

1. **Opening Shot:** A smiling patient confidently showing off their new Dental Implants to the camera. Text overlay: "Regain your confidence with Dental Implants".

2. **Scene Transition:** The Dental Office logo and name, perhaps with a voiceover welcoming viewers to the practice.

3. **Scene 1:** A Dentist in a lab coat, standing in a brightly lit, clean Dental Office, introducing themselves and the topic of Dental Implants.

4. **Scene 2:** The Dentist explains what Dental Implants are, while a simple animation or graphics on the screen illustrate the key points.

5. **Scene 3:** Close-up shots of Dental Implant models. The Dentist continues to explain the benefits of Dental Implants over other tooth replacement options.

6. **Scene 4:** Real-life photos or videos showing the transformation of patients who have received Dental Implants at the clinic, accompanied by testimonial voiceovers from the patients.

7. **Scene 5:** The Dentist talks about the process of getting Dental Implants. This could include footage of the Dentist examining a patient, a patient in the Dental chair (showing that the procedure is comfortable and safe), and the final result of the procedure.

8. **Scene 6:** The Dentist reassures the viewers about the safety and longevity of Dental Implants, while text highlights and testimonials scroll on the screen.

9. **Closing Shot:** The Dentist invites viewers to schedule a consultation to see if Dental Implants are right for them. Contact information for the Dental Office appears on the screen.

10. **Final Transition:** Fade out to the Dental Office logo and tagline, perhaps with a reminder about scheduling a consultation.

In conclusion, while creating a video marketing strategy requires effort and creativity, the payoff can be significant. Begin small, test different formats, and let your content take center stage. Remember, even with limited resources, you can still make impactful videos. With just your phone and a great idea, you can revolutionize the way the world perceives your Dental Practice. As Brené Brown once said, "Vulnerability is the birthplace of innovation, creativity, and change". So, embrace the challenge, take the plunge, and let the magic of video marketing work wonders for your Dental Practice.

CHAPTER 9: THE ART OF VIDEO MARKETING FOR COSMETIC DENTISTRY AND IMPLANT DENTISTRY

"The best marketing doesn't feel like marketing."

~ Tom Fishburne

Cosmetic Dentistry and Implant Dentistry, two of the most artistically engaging branches of the Dental industry, undoubtedly need a marketing approach as artistically appealing. With the projected growth of the Cosmetic Dentistry market expected to reach $32.73 Billion by 2026, it is only sensible for practices to hone their marketing strategies, particularly video marketing, to attract a substantial chunk of this burgeoning market.

In this chapter, we will delve into the importance of video marketing in Cosmetic and Implant Dentistry, types of videos to produce, and methods for repurposing video content to optimize your returns on your video marketing investment.

From Problems To Solutions: Using the AIDA Method For Winning Dental Videos

The AIDA method is a tested marketing strategy that stands for attention, interest, desire, and action. This technique is instrumental in relating to the viewer's problems, creating empathy, and positioning your service as the solution to their issues, hence driving them towards a call-to-action.

In the context of Cosmetic and Implant Dentistry, the AIDA method becomes particularly effective as most patients in these domains are seeking solutions to their concerns about their smile, making it an emotional engagement. This chapter will guide you on using the AIDA method effectively in your video marketing strategies, including grabbing attention, retaining interest, stimulating desire, and driving viewers to action.

What Types of Videos to Create

The AIDA method can be used to create diverse video content for every service you offer. Some of the most popular Cosmetic procedures that you could consider for your video content are Teeth Whitening, Porcelain Veneers, Dental Implants, Smile Makeovers, Same-Day Dental Crowns, and Cosmetic Bonding.

You can make videos about each of your services and embed them on their relevant service pages on your website. This strategy would improve your search engine rankings as Google favors video content. Also, this will enhance the user experience on your website, leading to longer session duration times, a key factor in Search Engine Optimization (SEO).

Repurpose for Maximum ROI

Video marketing provides the flexibility to repurpose your video content in multiple ways. You can embed your videos on your website, share them on Social Media, include them in your email newsletters, air them on local TV, or even use them on streaming services and local movie theaters.

This chapter also provides valuable advice on maximizing the reach and impact of your video content, such as boosting your video's initial views on YouTube through your email newsletters and ensuring high-quality content for use on TV and streaming services.

Your Cosmetic and Implant Dentistry practice needs to shine amidst a myriad of other service providers. Video marketing provides you an opportunity to demonstrate why prospective patients should trust you with their Dental care. Using dynamic before and after imagery, patient testimonials, procedure walk-throughs, and educational content, you can attract and engage your audience.

The use of engaging and meaningful visual content in Dental Marketing not only entices potential patients but also educates and reassures them about the treatments and procedures offered by your practice. According to a study by the Social Science Research Network, 65% of people are visual learners, making a powerful case for the use of imagery and video content in your marketing efforts. As mentioned, before and after images can vividly demonstrate the transformative impact of your Dental services, thereby bolstering the confidence of potential patients.

Similarly, patient testimonials provide social proof and enhance the credibility of your practice - Nielsen reports that 92% of consumers trust organic, user-generated content more than they trust traditional advertising. Furthermore, procedure walk-throughs help demystify the Dental process, potentially alleviating anxieties and increasing the likelihood of appointment bookings. The rising popularity of educational content in digital marketing strategies, which according to Optinmonster can help boost traffic by up to 200%, indicates that audiences appreciate and respond to useful, informative content. Therefore, by leveraging these forms of visual content, you can create a well-rounded and highly effective Dental Marketing strategy.

As you leverage the tips and techniques in this chapter, and throughout this book, you'll build an effective video marketing strategy that will position your Dental Practice as an industry leader, attuned to its patients' needs and desires.

CHAPTER 10: BREAK THE STAGE FRIGHT TO SPEAK CONFIDENTLY ON CAMERA

"Feel the fear and do it anyway."

~ Susan Jeffers

Public speaking is one of the most common fears people have, and that fear can magnify exponentially when you're speaking on camera. In this chapter, we'll explore a few strategies to help you feel more confident and natural in front of the camera. Whether you're a seasoned speaker or a first-time video star, these tips can help you appear poised, knowledgeable, and engaging to your audience.

Know Your Material:

1. The first step towards feeling confident on camera is knowing your material. This doesn't mean you have to memorize a script word for word, but you should understand your topic deeply. You should know the key points you want to hit, and be able to speak about them conversationally. If you need to, it's perfectly okay to use notes or a teleprompter to help you remember what you want to say.

Practice Makes Perfect:

2. Practice as much as you can before your filming day. You can rehearse in front of a mirror, or even better, use a camera or your smartphone to record yourself. This allows you to see how you look and sound on camera, and lets you identify areas where you might want to improve.

Body Language:

3. Your body language can communicate as much, if not more, than your words. Stand tall, keep your shoulders back and relax. This not only makes you look confident but also helps you feel more confident. Practice using hand gestures to emphasize your points but be careful not to overdo it. Remember to smile and maintain eye contact with the camera as if it's a person you're talking to.

Voice Control:

4. How you speak is just as important as what you say. Speak clearly and at a moderate pace, taking care to articulate your words. Practice modulating your voice to emphasize important points and to keep your delivery interesting.

Wardrobe and Makeup:

5. Wear clothes that make you feel comfortable and confident. However, also be aware of how they will look on camera. Avoid bright colors, patterns, and jewelry that can distract from your message. As for makeup, a natural look is usually best, but you may want to use a little more than usual to counteract the camera's tendency to wash out your complexion.

Visualize Success:

6. Visualizing a successful outcome can help reduce anxiety. Take a few moments before you start filming to close your eyes and imagine yourself delivering your message confidently and effectively. Most great performers in business, sports and arts do this on a regular basis to help elevate their own performance.

Breathe:

7. Deep breathing can help calm nerves. Before you start recording, take a few moments to take some deep breaths, in through your nose and out through your mouth.

Accept Imperfection:

8. Nobody is perfect, and your audience isn't expecting perfection. In fact, a few minor mistakes can make you seem more human and relatable. If you make a mistake during filming, don't panic. Just take a moment to compose yourself, and then carry on.

Remember, the goal of your video is not to deliver a perfect performance, but to connect with your audience and communicate your message effectively. With practice and preparation, you'll find that speaking on camera becomes easier and even enjoyable.

"No matter how much experience you have, there's always something new you can learn and room for improvement."

~ Roy T. Bennett

Finally, be patient with yourself. It's normal to feel a bit uncomfortable in front of the camera when you're starting out. With each video you create, you'll gain confidence and improve your skills. And remember, the most important thing is stay present and do the best you can when capturing this content. Surround yourself with uplifting people who always encourage you to try new things, be creative and have confidence in your ability to craft powerful content.

CHAPTER 11: HARNESSING VIDEO MARKETING TO AMPLIFY YOUR ONLINE PERSONA AND FOSTER PROFOUND RELATIONSHIPS WITH YOUR PATIENTS

Congratulations! You've conquered your trepidations about recording videos for your Dental practice and have finally taken the first step. So, what's next?

Even after wrapping up the recording day, there's a substantial amount of work to do. The subsequent stage involves promoting your videos to your existing and potential clients, ensuring that your hard work doesn't vanish into oblivion. With adept strategies, you can convert your videos into potent marketing tools. These resources will help maintain a healthy inflow of clients interacting with your Dental Practice and booking appointments.

In this chapter, we will provide some excellent strategies on how and where to promote your videos, ensuring maximum visibility and commendable ROI on your video marketing efforts and time investment.

The Ideal Platforms for Posting Your Videos

The platform on which you publish your videos carries significant importance. Understanding the type of videos suitable for each platform is crucial when using various online platforms like your website, Facebook, Instagram, TikTok, LinkedIn, YouTube, and Twitter. You also need to consider what works best for each channel. As not all social media channels are the same, audiences on each platform typically have different content expectations.

For instance, LinkedIn may be more suitable for high-quality video content compared to impromptu live videos. YouTube is perfect for extensive explainers and tutorials, while Facebook, Instagram, and TikTok are ideal for listicles. Short-format, easily consumable content is great for these platforms, especially when you wish to go live and engage your audience directly.

Short-format videos are currently emerging as the most popular style of content to record and repurpose across platforms. These videos, when created correctly, will be the most efficient to produce and the most impactful part of your video marketing efforts.

Blogs also serve as an excellent platform to share your video content. If you run a blog, it would be wise to embed your videos within your blog posts. Just ensure that the video content aligns with the blog content theme to ensure favorability from both website visitors and Google.

"No matter what you do, your job is to tell your story."

~ Gary Vaynerchuk

Here's a quick overview of what type of content performs best on your Social Media channels:

Having a posting strategy for each video before you begin recording is crucial. Knowing where you will post the video in advance can help you better engage with the specific audience during the filming process. You can essentially anticipate their needs and expectations based on the platform they are using.

"Without strategy, content is just stuff, and the world has enough stuff."

~ Arjun Basu

Innovative Ways to Leverage Your Videos

Modern Dental Practices can utilize numerous inventive platforms to interact with their patients on a more personal level. Video content marketing platforms allow you to create and host videos for various marketing scenarios and track viewer analytics as well as campaign success. Besides sharing your videos on Social Media sites and your website, consider exploring some of the video content marketing platforms mentioned below.

YouTube

YouTube continues to be the reigning champion in the video content sector. Apart from offering the perfect platform to optimize and upload your videos, you can also run targeted YouTube Ads.

The combination of YouTube Advertising with quality video content opens massive opportunities for your Dental Practice's marketing success! Like all paid ad initiatives, it's crucial to have an experienced professional run these and constantly track analytics, insights, and ROI.

Moreover, maintaining a YouTube presence can enhance your visibility in Google searches since videos hosted on YouTube are prioritized in Google's search results. Given that Google owns YouTube and that it's the world's second-largest search engine, YouTube should be your first choice for content posting.

Why YouTube Works

The Answer Lies in the Numbers

Recent statistics indicate that YouTube has 2.3 billion users worldwide. This amounts to about four times the population of North America. Daily, viewers watch over one billion hours of video on the platform, generating billions of views. If every person on Earth watched YouTube videos, it would translate to roughly 8.4 minutes per person per day.

Having an active YouTube channel for your Dental Practice is crucial! A Pew Research study suggests that 81% of Americans use YouTube compared to 69% who use Facebook. Furthermore, YouTube continues to witness substantial growth worldwide, particularly with the trend of cord-cutting.

The Logistics

Fortunately, setting up a YouTube channel is straightforward, so don't let this phase daunt you. To launch a YouTube channel for your Dental Practice, you need a Google account. It's advised that you either link your business email to your YouTube account or, if multiple people will be uploading content, create a practice-specific email for YouTube-related tasks.

Upon setting up your Google account and accessing your YouTube channel, you can tailor your Practice's channel to reflect your branding and preferences. Ensure that your channel aligns with any existing Practice branding to provide a seamless marketing experience and build recognition for your audience.

Uploading videos is relatively simple, but the key lies in proper optimization before publishing. After saving them on your phone or desktop, uploading is as simple as clicking a button. We strongly recommend that you add an engaging title and a description of at least 250 words to enhance your video's appeal and search rankings. If you know your Practice's SEO keywords, this is a good place to logically use keywords in titles and descriptions to enhance your visibility in searches.

The video title should also be strategic and related to the specific search term you are trying to rank for. For instance, if the video content is from a patient testimonial on the Dental Implants procedure and your practice is in Madison, WI, this could be the title:

Dental Implants in Madison WI (Patient Testimonial)

You should also add tags to enhance your video's visibility and categorize your videos into different sections as you amass a library. For instance, you may have how-to videos, patient testimonials, team interviews, procedure highlights, and more.

Thinking of YouTube like "HowTube" is a wise way to proceed with your content on this powerful platform. We see YouTube being an absolute game-changer for our clients when leveraged properly.

"Create videos with a distinct purpose. Anticipate your ideal consumer's needs and create content to address those needs." ~ Brian Rotsztein

To effectively engage visitors on your Dental website, it's paramount to feature your most compelling video content prominently on your homepage. Video content has a proven impact on visitor behavior, with statistics indicating a significant surge in conversion rates - as high as 80% - merely by embedding a single video on a website's homepage. An 80% increase in conversions can make a substantial difference to any business, let alone one in the Dental field. This implies that prospective patients not only enjoy video content but also find it persuasive enough to commit to your services.

Furthermore, incorporating video content throughout your website can lead to visitors spending more time exploring what you have to offer. On average, websites utilizing videos across various pages experience an impressive 88% increase in time spent by visitors. This extended interaction can enhance visitors' understanding of your services, provide them with in-depth insights into your Dental practices, and create a more personal connection with your brand.

YouTube Advertising

As mentioned, YouTube and Google provide a powerful suite of marketing tools at your disposal. Regular use of these tools to your advantage can help build awareness, attract new patients, and boost office revenues.

YouTube Ads allow you to integrate your Dental Practice messaging before or during videos. You are likely familiar with these ads if you've spent time on YouTube. They come in many formats, including ads to build awareness, drive consideration, or induce action. YouTube's Ad platform can guide you through the available options and how to set them up. These ads can be skippable or non-skippable and can include Call-To-Action buttons to guide the audience directly to your Dental Website to learn more or book an appointment.

After creating a video, YouTube's advertising platform will guide you through the campaign setup. This includes setting your advertising budget and target audience. Once the campaign is live, you can easily track your campaign results on your YouTube Advertising account and make necessary adjustments.

Collaborate with Other Dental Professionals

Collaboration can be a great way to boost your video exposure. Reach out to other Dental professionals for video collaborations. You could interview each other or collaborate on educational content. Not only will this benefit your audience by providing them with more valuable content, but it also gives you access to a whole new audience base.

Host Webinars and Live Q&A Sessions

Webinars and live Q&A sessions allow you to interact with your audience directly. This can help you establish strong relationships with your audience. Remember to promote these sessions beforehand on your social media channels and your website, and consider partnering with relevant influencers or professionals to bring additional value to your audience.

Embed Videos in Email Newsletters

If you have a list of email subscribers, embedding your videos in newsletters can be an effective way to boost exposure. Make sure to add a compelling subject line to attract clicks. Studies have shown that including the word "video" in an email subject line increases open rates.

Utilize Influencer Marketing

Influencer marketing can be an effective way to increase exposure. Connect with relevant influencers in your niche and collaborate on a video project. The influencer can share your video with their followers, dramatically increasing your video's exposure. For most practices, these would be considered "micro influencers" in your local community, rather than Justin Bieber.

Feature Real Patients and Their Testimonials

Patient testimonials are a powerful marketing tool. If your patients are comfortable, consider featuring them in your videos. This not only adds credibility to your videos but also makes them more relatable to potential patients.

Consistency is Key

Remember that consistent effort over time is more valuable than sporadic, high-intensity bursts. Consistency in video production and promotion will help you build a loyal audience over time. Consider creating a content calendar to schedule your video production and promotion activities.

Seek Professional Help If Required

Lastly, remember that there's no shame in seeking professional help if needed. Video marketing can be complex, and a professional digital marketing agency or consultant can provide valuable guidance and expertise.

The Bottom Line

The transformative potential of video marketing is undeniable in the sphere of comprehensive marketing strategy. Not only does it offer an avenue to connect more profoundly with your audience, but it also enables the provision of informative, engaging content that draws new patients while securing the loyalty of existing ones. But it doesn't stop there. Videos also allow you to bring your Dental Practice's mission and personality to life, helping to form a more emotional and relatable bond with your audience. Therefore, as you navigate your video marketing endeavors, remember that providing value to your audience is paramount. In the process, you should aim to humanize your Dental Practice, showcasing the care, skill, and dedication that sets you apart in this field. This is the bottom line to an effective video marketing strategy - connecting, engaging, and delivering true value.

Remember, "In a world where you can be anything, be a brand."

~ B.J. Cook

Ready to dive into the exciting world of video marketing? With these best practices, you're well on your way to making the most of your video content, boosting your online persona, and fostering profound relationships with your patients.

CHAPTER 12: THAT'S A WRAP - CREATING A HIGH-POWERED POST-FILMING DENTAL MARKETING STRATEGY

"Video marketing is a powerful tool because videos can be repurposed over and over again to attract endless amounts of organic, social, and paid search traffic. A single video can be transformed into an audio podcast, blog post, infographic, slideshow, lead magnet, Facebook ad, email newsletter, Twitter post, landing page content, and more."

~ Stephen Hockman

Wrapping Up Video Elements

In the fast-paced world of today, video content reigns supreme. As consumers seek information, learn new skills, or engage with brands, they lean increasingly towards video formats. Video content breathes life into a story in a way words on a page or a mailed flier can't – through colors, voices, music, and images. Videos provide an immersive way of sharing your Dental Practice's story, a critical element in a world shifting from written to more oral and visual forms of storytelling.

Video is an indispensable tool for Dental Practices aiming to keep up with the shifting digital landscape, one that's moving towards more innovative and complex formats, such as augmented and virtual reality environments. While today your practice might rely on videos to tell a compelling story, the future holds the potential for patients to experience your Dental Practice virtually or in the Metaverse.

If you haven't already embraced video in your marketing strategy, consider this a wake-up call. Video isn't a mere accessory in your marketing plan; it's a necessity for meeting your patients' expectations.

Patience is key in video optimization. It can take up to three months for Google to assign proper rankings in the Search Engine Results Pages (SERPs). However, if your Dental Practice is new to video marketing, you should start seeing relevant metrics within a few weeks of uploading your first videos. Following the strategies outlined in these chapters will accelerate this process, paving the way for you to reap the benefits of a well-structured video marketing strategy.

CHAPTER 13: DENTAL WEBSITES - MASTERING CONVERSION RATE OPTIMIZATION FOR NEW PATIENT GROWTH

"In the digital world, conversation is the catalyst for conversion."

~ Dan Roth

Conversion Rate Optimization (CRO) quantifies the success of your Dental website by tracking the ratio of visitors who become real-life patients. As an integral part of digital marketing, focusing on CRO should be paramount in your marketing efforts.

In general, websites in various industries average a CRO of 1%-3%. This implies that out of every 100 visits, roughly 1-3 customers or clients are converted. What if we could push this boundary and lift your Dental website's CRO to a staggering 5%-10%+? Such a transformation would significantly boost your practice's growth, even if all traffic and advertising dollars stayed the same.

At our agency, focusing on CRO for a client's website is our Top Priority for all marketing campaigns.

Below are some strategies to elevate your website's CRO:

Elevating Your CRO: A Comprehensive Guide

1. The CRO of your website largely depends on the quality and relevance of the content you present. This section elaborates on the critical elements that you should incorporate into your website design and content strategy.

Prime Real Estate: Above the Fold

The top section of a website, visible without scrolling down, is termed 'Above The Fold'. This zone is the first impression for your potential patients and hence a critical determinant of conversion rates. Therefore, selecting a competent and skilled website developer who understands the importance of this area is crucial.

Prompting Action: The Call-To-Action

When visitors arrive at your website, what do you want them to do next? Usually, you want them to schedule an appointment. Therefore, having visible Call-To-Action (CTA) buttons with phrases like "BOOK MY APPOINTMENT" is recommended. Using the word "MY" personalizes the action and makes it more inviting, thereby improving CRO. Experiment with various fonts, colors, and placements to optimize your CTA.

Visual Cues: CRO Header Images

A well-selected website header image can guide your visitors towards your CTA buttons. A Dentist interacting with a patient in the image, for example, should be positioned such that they are looking towards each other, not directly at the viewer. Position your CTA button along the line of their gaze. It may seem subtle, but these visual cues significantly influence viewer attention and thus CRO.

Although it's a virtual experience, most people don't want to be looked at. So make sure to direct the attention of eyelines towards your desired CTA buttons. This alone will have a huge impact on your overall CRO performance.

Building Trust: Trust Signals

Highlight your affiliations with various Dental Associations and ongoing education organizations by placing their logos on your website's homepage. Known as Trust Signals, these logos reassure potential patients and improve your CRO. Ideally, you want to add so many that they scroll from left-to-right across the screen. Have your website designer source each of these logos, then change the color palette to match your brand identity to give the website a more clean, polished look. Whenever possible to add fresh Trust Signals to your website, please go ahead and keep building this section. Overtime, it'll become a major aspect of your website's success.

Modernize Booking: Online Scheduling Feature

Just as restaurants have streamlined their reservation process with online booking, Dental practices can greatly benefit from implementing an online scheduling system. An efficient scheduling platform that integrates with your Practice Management System (PMS) and allows for online form submission not only increases your CRO but also aids in efficient management.

At our agency, we are huge fans of NexHealth for online scheduling. Their feature integrates with your PMS system, while also being super user friendly for both front office personnel and patients trying to book appointments. Regardless of the types of patients you are looking to attract, implementing online scheduling is an absolute must in today's digital world.

Embracing the digital shift with online scheduling significantly enhances your practice's accessibility. According to Accenture, 77% of patients consider the ability to book, change, or reschedule appointments online as crucial. Therefore, a smooth, easy-to-navigate scheduling platform can be a key determinant in a patient's decision to choose your practice over others.

NexHealth stands out due to its seamless integration with your Practice Management System, intuitive interface, and its capacity to handle real-time availability, which in turn minimizes double bookings and streamlines administrative duties. This makes the entire appointment booking process less tedious for both your team and your patients.

Furthermore, online scheduling platforms like NexHealth offer the convenience of 24/7 accessibility. As a result, potential patients can make appointments outside of regular office hours, making your services accessible to a wider audience. As per a survey conducted by GetApp, 70% of customers prefer to book online as compared to a phone call, illustrating the rising demand for such a feature.

Remember, the initial interaction a patient has with your practice, often booking an appointment, sets the tone for their entire customer journey. By prioritizing ease and efficiency through a tool like online scheduling, you show your patients that you value their time and convenience. It's a strategic move that speaks volumes about your practice's commitment to providing exceptional customer service, even before a patient steps into your clinic.

In the age of digitalization, adopting an online scheduling system is not just a strategic business decision but a necessity. After all, in the words of Bill Gates, "The first rule of any technology used in a business is that automation applied to an efficient operation will magnify the efficiency." So why not embrace technology that amplifies efficiency and enhances patient experience?

Highlight Successes: Before & After Images

Showcase your skills with a well-curated Smile Gallery featuring before and after images. Consistently capture and update these images while ensuring patient consent. These visuals increase trust and thus aid in conversion. You always want to showcase real patients, rather than relying on stock imagery for this super important form of content. Also, sets of four images that include full face images can help showcase these beautiful smiles even more.

Boosting Referrals: Refer a Friend

Make the most of existing patient relationships by incorporating a "Refer a Friend" feature on your website. This feature should be easily accessible and allow for easy submission of the referring patient's and the referred person's details.

Encouraging Feedback: Review Our Practice

Frequent Google reviews on your Google My Business (GMB) listing are vital for local SEO, driving website traffic, and increasing new patients. Automate the feedback request process to amplify review collection and improve your CRO.

Transparency in Payment: Financial Options

Ensure clarity about your financial options to reduce queries and improve direct bookings. Encourage potential patients to reach out with any questions about payment options.

Data-Driven Decisions: Google Analytics

Implement Google Analytics on your website to gain insights about visitor behavior and trends. Use these data to improve your marketing strategies.

Google Analytics is a powerful tool that allows you to make data-driven decisions for your Dental practice. By implementing Google Analytics on your website, you gain invaluable insights into visitor behavior and trends, allowing you to fine-tune your marketing strategies accordingly.

Why Google Analytics?

Google Analytics is an essential asset for any digital marketer. With the vast amount of data it provides, it can help you understand your audience better. You can see who visits your website (demographics like age, gender, location), how they get there (via search engines, social media, direct links), what pages they visit, how long they stay, and much more. This information allows you to see what's working and what isn't, providing the knowledge needed to improve and optimize your strategies.

Insights from Google Analytics

When you delve into Google Analytics, you'll find a wealth of information that can drive your Dental marketing strategies. For instance:

- **Bounce Rate:** This indicates the percentage of visitors who leave your website after viewing only one page. A high bounce rate might suggest that the page isn't engaging enough or doesn't contain the information visitors are looking for.

- **Traffic Sources:** Understanding where your traffic comes from can help you determine which of your marketing strategies are most effective. If a lot of traffic comes from social media, for instance, it might be worth investing more in your social media marketing efforts.

- **User Flow:** This shows the path visitors take through your website. This can help identify any potential roadblocks that might be causing users to leave your website prematurely.

- **Conversion Goals:** Google Analytics allows you to set specific goals (like form submissions or appointment bookings) to track how many visitors complete these desired actions. Monitoring these conversions is essential for measuring the success of your marketing strategies.

By examining these metrics, you can discern patterns, identify strengths and weaknesses in your website's design and content, and make the necessary adjustments.

Implementing Changes Based on Data

Once you have these insights, it's important to act on them. Data-driven decisions allow you to allocate your marketing budget effectively, improve user experience, and ultimately attract and retain more patients. If the data shows that a specific service page is attracting a lot of visitors, for example, consider enhancing that page with more detailed information, patient testimonials, or a call-to-action to book an appointment.

In summary, Google Analytics is an essential tool in the modern digital marketing toolkit. The insights it provides allows you to refine your marketing strategies, improve user engagement, and ultimately grow your Dental practice. Remember, data is only as valuable as the decisions it drives. With Google Analytics, you have a wealth of data at your fingertips - use it wisely.

Ensuring Speed: Website Speed

Maintain a fast website loading speed to improve user experience and CRO. Regularly check your website speed and address any issues that could slow down loading time. Websites such as GTMetrix.com are easy to use and figure out your website speed. Make sure to test your website speed on a regular basis and fix any problems that may arise.

Website speed, or how quickly users can see and interact with content, is a crucial element of user experience. It directly impacts your practice's online visibility, patient satisfaction, and ultimately, your conversion rates. Google, in its research, found that as page load time goes from 1s to 3s, the probability of a visitor bouncing increases by 32%. It only gets worse with further delay, skyrocketing to 123% as the load time reaches 10s. In a world where patience is scarce, a slow website could mean losing potential patients to faster, more responsive competitors.

Utilizing tools like GTMetrix can help identify issues hindering your website's speed. This service analyzes your site's speed performance using PageSpeed and YSlow scores, providing detailed reports and recommendations to improve load times. However, merely knowing your website's speed is not enough. You must be proactive in addressing identified issues. This could involve optimizing your images, minimizing HTTP requests, reducing server response time, enabling browser caching, or minifying CSS, JavaScript, and HTML.

Moreover, it's essential to realize that website speed is not a one-time fix but requires ongoing attention. Regular monitoring and tweaking can help maintain optimal speed, ensuring a smooth and satisfying user experience. A study by Akamai found that a 100-millisecond delay in website load time can decrease conversion rates by 7%. This illustrates the immense value of a speedy website in fostering positive user experiences and increasing conversion rates.

In essence, your website speed is the first impression you make on a prospective patient. In the words of acclaimed author Malcolm Gladwell, "We don't know where our first impressions come from or precisely what they mean, so we don't always appreciate their fragility." Ensuring that this first digital impression is a great one can significantly influence a potential patient's journey with your Dental Practice.

Smooth Navigation: User Experience Basics

A well-optimized website that is easy to navigate, mobile-friendly, clear in descriptions, responsive to customer service queries, and thoughtful in content design significantly enhances user experience, leading to increased conversion rates.

In the fiercely competitive Dental industry, a compelling online presence is more crucial than ever. Your website is much more than an information portal; it is your digital storefront, often creating the first impression for potential patients. As such, it's critical that your website is user-friendly, mobile-responsive, and filled with clear, meaningful content.

Renowned business strategist Michael Porter once said, "The essence of strategy is choosing what not to do." This quote underscores the importance of strategic decision-making when designing your Dental website. Every design choice, content inclusion, or interactive feature should be implemented with your target audience in mind. According to Statista, over half of all website traffic was generated through mobile phones. This means that optimizing your website for mobile usage isn't just a desirable feature, it's a strategic necessity.

Clear and concise content does more than just inform. It enhances user experience, elevates your website's search engine rankings, and amplifies your practice's visibility to potential patients. By ensuring your website content caters to the needs of your patient demographic, your website becomes more than a digital business card - it becomes a persuasive platform for your Dental services.

In the sphere of customer service, every point of interaction, be it an inquiry form, a live chat or a phone call facilitated through your website, is an opportunity to impress and engage. A comprehensive study by PwC reveals that 73% of all people consider customer experience as an essential factor in their purchasing decisions. By providing prompt, informative, and courteous responses to inquiries, you're not only solving immediate issues but also fostering a robust relationship with potential patients.

Adopting and consistently applying these recommendations may not yield immediate results, but they will undoubtedly increase your Dental Website's Conversion Rate Optimization over time, attracting more patients and promoting sustainable growth for your practice. As you undertake the task of optimizing your website, remember the wisdom imparted by marketing guru Seth Godin: "Don't find customers for your products, find products for your customers." This patient-centric approach is the key to your success - understanding your patients' needs, meeting and exceeding their expectations, and ultimately delivering valuable and gratifying experiences. Remember, every detail counts, every enhancement matters, and every satisfied patient contributes to the continued success of your Dental practice.

By understanding and implementing these recommendations, you can increase your Dental Website's Conversion Rate Optimization, bringing in more patients and improving your practice's overall growth.

CHAPTER 14: KEYWORD OPTIMIZATION - UPLIFTING USER EXPERIENCE AND ONLINE SUCCESS

"Marketing's job is never done. It's about perpetual motion. We must continue to innovate every day."

- Beth Comstock

Keywords, keyword phrases, and the way we use them have evolved significantly, but their core importance remains. They guide potential patients and visitors to your Dental Practice online and enhance user experience.

To thrive in this ever-evolving landscape, Dental Practices must keep up with emerging trends, such as the growth of voice search and the constant need to optimize conversion rates. This chapter presents a guide to achieving these goals.

Mastering Keyword Usage:

1. Online keyword finders can help you identify popular and relevant keywords for your practice. Place these strategically in your content to aid users in finding your website, consequently improving user experience. Although, you should have a fairly basic understanding of the keywords you want to specifically target and rank for. Along with your head of marketing, constantly work on this list together and make sure it's comprehensive, yet targeted.

Conversational Content for Voice Search:

2. Voice search is revolutionizing customer queries. Therefore, creating content that aligns with conversational language is vital. Consider how questions are asked verbally to create content that resonates with voice searches.

Back to Basics: CRO Optimization:

3. Sometimes, revisiting the fundamentals can lead to the most significant improvements. Seek honest feedback from your patients and leverage this valuable information to optimize your conversion rates.

The Power of Feedback:

4. Active communication with your patients and social media followers can provide you with invaluable insights. Encourage users to leave feedback and reviews, as these greatly influence potential patients. Making sure the review request feedback is properly automated is instrumental to the quality and quantity of your social proof.

Deploy Surveys:

5. Surveys can be a useful tool for collecting detailed feedback from patients. These can cover various aspects from their visit experience to their suggestions for new services. Regularly conducting these surveys can provide ongoing insight into your practice.

Understanding User Searches:

6. Tools such as Google Search Console can help you understand what users are searching for. These insights can inform your website content strategy, making it more relevant and effective. Every website needs to have a corresponding Google Search Console account to help better manage all aspects of your online presence.

Enhancing Trustworthiness:

7. Your online reputation can significantly influence your success. Building and strengthening this reputation should be a strategic priority. Consistently providing value and reliable service will improve your trust factor. Most importantly, focusing on your Google My Business listing should be top priority here.

Consistency is Crucial:

8. Maintaining consistency across all platforms is key to building trust and identity. This consistency should extend to the narrative, logo, colors, and tone of communication. Addressing queries and responding to negative comments with transparency will further improve your image.

Social Listening:

9. Social listening is an effective way to manage your reputation and identify potential pain points. Regularly monitoring and engaging with comments on your social media platforms can help you address issues swiftly and highlight your commitment to customer service. The quicker you communicate with individuals leaving comments or reviews, the better chances you have of elevating your overall brand identity.

By mastering these elements of digital marketing—keyword optimization, voice search content, and conversion rate optimization— is akin to laying the foundation for a skyscraper. With a strong and resilient base, you are well-equipped to weather any changes in the digital landscape and poised to reach for new heights in your Dental Practice.

As Microsoft's CEO Satya Nadella astutely observed, "We are moving from a world where computing power was scarce to a place where it now is almost limitless, and where the true scarce commodity is increasingly human attention." In a world teeming with content, capturing and maintaining the attention of potential patients is indeed a significant challenge. Yet, it's one you can overcome by staying attuned to evolving search trends and continually refining your digital marketing strategies.

Research from Google underscores the importance of keeping pace with these trends. For example, it has been found that over 20% of mobile queries are voice searches. By creating content tailored for voice search, you're positioning your practice to be discovered by this growing demographic of users.

Meanwhile, consider that Econsultancy reports only about 22% of businesses are satisfied with their conversion rates. Clearly, there is a massive opportunity for growth in this area, and by committing to ongoing conversion rate optimization, your practice can be among the elite businesses that capitalize on this potential.

In closing, remember that the field of digital marketing, much like the field of Dentistry, is one of constant change and advancement. Embrace this reality, and view it not as a challenge, but as an opportunity for continuous learning, growth, and improvement. The strategies you've learned in this chapter are not one-time tasks but ongoing processes. They form the bedrock of your digital presence, and their ongoing execution and refinement will play an instrumental role in the continued growth and success of your Dental Practice for years to come.

With the right approach and mindset, as former Facebook COO Sheryl Sandberg famously said, "Done is better than perfect." Emphasize progress over perfection and be prepared to learn from each success and setback. After all, your digital marketing journey is just like your Dental Practice: it's not simply about reaching a destination—it's about the continual pursuit of excellence.

CHAPTER 15: EMBRACING VOICE-BASED APPS FOR CRO AND BRAND VISIBILITY

"Make the prospect a more informed buyer with content."

- Robert Simon

The proliferation of voice-based apps such as Siri and Alexa has revolutionized the way people manage their lives. These apps are now a vital part of everyday routines, from cooking to shopping, and they're here to stay. For Dental Practices, voice-based apps offer promising opportunities for enhancing Conversion Rate Optimization (CRO) and increasing brand visibility.

The Power of Voice-Based Apps:

1. Voice-based apps are gradually becoming the multitaskers in our lives, simplifying tasks and saving time. With the increased adoption of these apps, Dental practices must align their strategies to leverage this growing trend.

Enhancing CRO with Voice-Based Apps:

2. Voice-based apps can be a powerful tool for improving your Dental Practice's CRO. By ensuring your content is optimized for voice search, you make your practice more accessible and visible to a broader audience, consequently enhancing conversion rates.

Increasing Brand Visibility:

3. Embracing voice-based apps can significantly increase your brand visibility. As more people rely on voice-based apps for searches,

ensuring your Dental Practice is easily found through voice search can help boost your brand's visibility.

Both SEO and CRO are essential components of a successful Dental Practice's online presence. They share a common goal of enhancing your website's performance, content, and structure, crucial to Local SEO. If your website is outdated or slow to load, it will negatively impact your SEO efforts and the success rate of new patient acquisition.

Your website, often the first point of contact for potential patients, needs to be modern, fresh, and user-friendly. In the following chapter, we will delve into the intricacies of Local SEO for your Dental Practice, providing you with the knowledge to ensure your Dental Practice website stands out in local search results.

Keep in mind that only 3% of searchers ever click past the first page. That means even small SEO improvements could result in more web traffic and better new patient results. More reason to constantly be tracking your website rankings, overall new patient numbers and inquiries your front desk is receiving.

Additionally, remember that your brand's visual identity—its logo, color scheme, typography, and overall design aesthetic—is not merely about aesthetics. It is a strategic tool that communicates your Dental Practice's values, mission, and personality, setting the stage for the kind of patient experience one can expect. Your website, as a digital extension of your brand, should seamlessly carry this narrative forward, warmly welcoming potential patients into the world of your practice.

In our rapidly digitizing world, a compelling and user-friendly website is not a luxury but a necessity. The way you present your practice online can significantly influence a potential patient's decision to choose your practice over another. So, take the time to ensure that your website accurately and compellingly represents your brand.

As we move to the next chapter on Local SEO for your Dental Practice, you'll discover how to maximize the visibility of your carefully crafted website in local search results, attracting more potential patients and enhancing your practice's growth and success. Hold tight, as the world of SEO is a fascinating one, full of potential for your practice to reach new heights.

"SEO is not something you do anymore. It's what happens when you do everything else right."

- Chad Pollitt

CHAPTER 16: MASTERING LOCAL SEO AND MAXIMIZING YOUR GOOGLE PRESENCE

"Content is the atomic particle of all digital marketing."

- Rebecca Lieb

A key aspect of Dental Practice SEO is targeting your local community. As Dental Practices are local businesses, investing extra effort in local search engine optimization can yield great dividends. However, the secret lies in keeping your website information up-to-date, including contact details, to prevent harming your local SEO.

Importance of SEO for Dental Practice:

1. SEO is a fundamental component of online success for Dental Practices. In today's competitive environment, smart SEO tactics and etiquette are necessary, as search engines like Google have tightened the rules, penalizing old practices like keyword stuffing.

Google Ranking Explained:

2. Understanding how Google ranks pages is essential. Typically, paid ads appear at the top of the page, followed by organic results. Both organic traffic (from SEO) and paid traffic (SEM or PPC) are crucial for Dental Practices. The key is to be showing for both paid and organic search results, in your community, for the specific inquiries you are wanting.

Increasing Google Reviews and Social Proof:

3. Increasing Google Reviews on your Google My Business (GMB) listing is vital for outranking local competition. As mentioned, an automated review request process for your Dental Patients can enhance the frequency and visibility of reviews on your GMB listing.

How SEO Works:

4. Google uses complex algorithms to rank pages, considering factors such as quality backlinks, content, and page structure. Emphasizing these aspects in your SEO strategy can greatly improve your online presence.

SEO Basics and Techniques:

5. Understanding SEO basics like optimizing your Google My Business listing, incorporating Google 360 Virtual Tour, video marketing, and keyword research can boost your Dental Website's visibility and patient acquisition.

Content Marketing and On-Page Optimization:

6. Creating quality, unique content with appropriate keywords and optimizing your page structure can significantly enhance your SEO ranking. Constantly be working to improve your website's content, reflecting all of the news and updates at your office.

Site Architecture Optimization and Semantic Markup:

7. Internal linking and semantic markups are additional ways to improve your site's SEO. These techniques help search engines better understand and discover your website's content.

SEO Tools for Your Dental Practice:

8. Leveraging SEO Tools like Google Search Console, Google Tag Manager, Google Ads Keyword Planner, backlink analysis tools, and SEO platforms can enhance your SEO efforts and provide valuable insights.

"Google only loves you when everyone else loves you first."

Wendy Piersall

By now, you should have a firm understanding of SEO and its importance for your Dental Practice. Remember, your website serves as the first point of contact with your patients - make it count. Indeed, a solid grasp of SEO is paramount to the success of your Dental Practice in today's digital era. As the primary touchpoint for potential patients, your website does more than just represent your practice—it serves as the foundation for your online presence and a critical element in your marketing arsenal.

Remember, it's not merely about making your website visible; it's about making it valuable. Moreover, don't overlook the influence of behavioral signals, such as click-through rates and mobile clicks to call. By providing a seamless user experience, you encourage positive user behaviors that, in turn, send positive signals to Google.

Harnessing the Power of Links for Page Rank

Website links, also known as "backlinks" in the world of Search Engine Optimization (SEO), are a crucial factor in search engine ranking. They serve as votes of confidence from other businesses and websites, boosting your website's credibility and authority. Given that most websites shy away from linking to poor-quality sites, Google uses these links as indicators of trust and relevance.

Building high-quality backlinks for your Dental Practice's website can significantly enhance your reputation and ranking in search engine results. This approach turns your website into a veritable game-changer in the realm of SEO. By reaching out and establishing relationships with businesses that complement your Dental Practice, you pave the way for potential link exchanges.

Increasing your website's authority and Google's "PageRank" involves seeking high-quality sites willing to share or link back to your content. Over the years, Google's PageRank algorithm has undergone thousands of updates, but the importance of quality backlinks has remained a constant factor. The higher the quality of your backlinks, the greater the SEO rewards you stand to reap.

For instance, consider joining your local Chamber of Commerce, which would usually offer a directory link back to your website. This creates a valuable local link, strengthening your local SEO efforts. In addition to this high-quality local link, membership in the Chamber of Commerce brings numerous other benefits, such as:

• Access to networking events • Additional sponsorship opportunities • The possibility of hosting events or business mixers at your practice • Featuring in their weekly email newsletters • And many more

Non-local links also hold great value. A prime example would be having your practice listed on the Kois Center directory of clinicians. As a highly reputable organization and website, a link from them would add immense value to your Dental Practice's website.

Securing Links: Remember to Ask!

Whether you're sponsoring an event, donating a product or service, or engaging in any offline opportunities, don't forget to inquire about a potential link from their website to yours. Accumulating these high-quality backlinks over time can have a transformative impact on your website's SEO strength. By making link-building an integral part of your marketing strategy, you lay the foundation for a stronger, more visible online presence for your Dental Practice.

In the dynamic world of Dental Marketing, one tool stands out as a game-changer: the Google 360 Virtual Tour. In our view, this feature is not just an enhancement, but an absolute necessity for any modern Dental Practice seeking to improve its Local SEO and overall Digital Footprint.

A Google 360 Virtual Tour leverages the power of immersive technology, allowing potential patients to virtually "walk-through" your Dental Practice right from the comfort of their homes. This gives them a sense of familiarity and trust before they ever step foot in your office. But it's not just the patients who benefit; Google's search algorithm loves this too. This interactive tool not only improves your visibility on Google Maps and Google Search, but it also increases user engagement and signals to Google that your website offers valuable content. This, in turn, significantly boosts your Local SEO ranking.

Moreover, a Google 360 Virtual Tour amplifies your overall Digital Footprint. It seamlessly integrates with other digital platforms, such as your website and social media profiles, thereby offering a holistic view of your Dental Practice. With this in your digital arsenal, you're not just promoting your practice; you're providing an interactive experience that sets you apart from the competition.

Simply put, embracing the Google 360 Virtual Tour as part of your Dental Marketing strategy could be the key to reaching more potential patients, improving their online experience, and ultimately, enhancing your practice's visibility and credibility in the digital space. This, we believe, is why it's an absolute must for your Dental Practice's ranking and overall Digital Footprint.

"As a marketer, if you're not using Google 360 yet, you're not marketing."
- A.C. Riley

In closing, SEO for your Dental Practice isn't a set-it-and-forget-it strategy—it's a continuous process of adaptation and improvement. Changes in algorithms, emerging technologies, and shifting user behaviors necessitate that SEO efforts be ongoing and evolving.

However, don't be daunted. With the foundations laid in this book, you are well-prepared to navigate the dynamic landscape of SEO. Remember, each optimization, no matter how small, is a step forward in enhancing your online visibility, attracting potential patients, and ultimately growing your Dental Practice. Embark on this journey with an open mind and a readiness to adapt. The path of SEO is not always straightforward, but each step you take will bring your Dental Practice closer to the pinnacle of online visibility and success.

As the renowned innovator, Thomas Edison once said, "There's a way to do it better - find it." Your pursuit of betterment in SEO is a testament to your commitment to your practice's growth. Let that be your motivation as you navigate the ever-changing landscape of digital marketing.

In the next chapter, we will dive deeper into the various strategies that can help you maximize your Dental Practice's online visibility and new patient acquisition.

CHAPTER 17: PPC FOR DENTAL MARKETING ROI - A WORD ABOUT GOOGLE ADWORDS

"Business has only two functions – marketing and innovation," said Milan Kundera, emphasizing the importance of platforms like Google AdWords in marketing. This pay-per-click advertising service is an indispensable tool for local businesses, especially Dental Practices seeking immediate online visibility and profitability.

AdWords, a product of Google's trillion-dollar empire, offers unparalleled efficiency and precision when managed correctly. It can instantly propel a Dental Practice to the top of search engine rankings, leading to a surge of new patient leads and appointment requests. Additionally, it can provide insights into your most effective SEO keywords, which can be incorporated into various digital assets, from website content to social media posts.

However, to unlock the full potential of Google AdWords, time and professional expertise are required. Therefore, delegating this task to a trained marketing professional is highly recommended.

PPC settings, like any powerful tool, must be handled with care. Mismanagement can lead to squandered spending. The most critical part of your targeting strategy is the LOCATION. Ensure your account manager understands the nuances of your specific geographic area, as this knowledge directly influences campaign success.

Insightful Tips for Using Google AdWords

1. Leverage the Keyword Planner: Google's Keyword Planner helps you discover keywords relevant to your Dental Practice. You can identify

search trends, see the average monthly search volume, and even get cost estimates for each keyword.

2. Utilize Negative Keywords: Negative keywords allow you to exclude irrelevant search terms from your campaigns. For instance, if you want to target people looking for "teeth whitening services," but not those searching for "DIY teeth whitening," "DIY" can be set as a negative keyword.

3. Implement Ad Extensions: Ad extensions can enhance your AdWords campaign by providing more information and additional reasons for people to choose your Dental Practice. Location extensions, call extensions, and site link extensions can all be beneficial.

4. Schedule Your Ads: Ad scheduling allows you to run your ads at times when they're most likely to convert. For example, if your Dental Office operates from 9 am to 5 pm, you might schedule your ads to run during these hours. Although, we encourage you to keep Google AdWords running at all times of the day. Statistics show that 40% of people who book online do this after hours, so having your Google AdWords campaigns enabled all times would be a must.

5. Monitor and Optimize: Continually monitor your campaign's performance. Make adjustments based on the data you gather to ensure your campaign's success. Google Analytics is a valuable tool for tracking and analyzing this data. Make sure to constantly be looking over your Google AdWords and Google Analytics insights with your marketing partner, along with comparing these data sets to overall performance with New Patients. This is crucially important for your overall marketing success.

PPC ad campaigns offer a myriad of benefits. They drive immediate traffic, are cost-effective, provide testing opportunities, and favor local businesses. As Henry Ford once noted, "Stopping advertising to save money is like stopping your watch to save time."

Setting clear, measurable goals is the cornerstone of a successful Google AdWords campaign. It all starts with a comprehensive keyword research process, aiming to understand what potential patients are searching for and how your practice can meet their needs. This includes identifying both high-volume search terms and niche, long-tail keywords that can attract a more targeted audience.

Setting parameters and goals helps to define what success looks like for your campaign. It may include increasing website traffic, driving more appointment bookings, or raising awareness of a specific Dental service. Therefore, it's crucial to establish key performance metrics that align with your goals. These might include click-through rates, cost per click, or conversion rates.

Furthermore, syncing your AdWords campaign with Google Analytics provides valuable insights into user behavior and campaign performance. This integration allows you to track how users interact with your website after clicking on your ads, providing data that can help optimize your campaigns and website for better results.

However, running a successful AdWords campaign isn't a "set it and forget it" task. It requires continuous testing, tweaking, and optimization. Regular A/B testing of different ad copy, keywords, and landing pages can help you understand what resonates with your audience and drives results.

The return on investment for Google AdWords can be significant. According to Google Economic Impact Report, businesses make an average of $2 in revenue for every $1 they spend on AdWords. Furthermore, considering that a lifelong patient's value can far exceed the initial acquisition cost, investing in PPC ads can offer a substantial return.

Yet, it's important to remember that AdWords is not a quick fix. It requires time, patience, and expertise to leverage its full potential. As Thomas Edison said, "Our greatest weakness lies in giving up. The most certain way to succeed is always to try just one more time." With persistence, data-driven decision making, and regular optimization, Google AdWords can prove to be a game-changer for your Dental Practice's marketing strategy.

CHAPTER 18: SOCIAL MEDIA FOR DENTISTS - WHAT SHOULD WE POST?

"Successful social media marketing is not built on impressions. It is built on relationships."

- Kim Garst

In this digital era, leveraging Social Media platforms effectively is not just an advantage but a necessity for your Dental Practice. The keyword in Social Media is indeed 'social.' It's a space for rapport building, relationship forming, storytelling, and brand expansion.

To kick off, always bear in mind that your Social Media platforms aren't just digital billboards. Instead, they are platforms that allow you to connect with your audience, engage them with valuable content, and build lasting relationships.

Embracing the Dynamic Nature of Social Media

Social Media is ever-changing, with new platforms emerging and algorithms constantly updating. Recognizing this dynamism is crucial to your social media strategy. Always be on the lookout for new trends and platforms that might be beneficial to your practice. Different platforms often attract different demographics, so consider who your target audience is and where they're most likely to spend their time online.

Are You Listening Socially?

Social Listening, or monitoring conversations around specific topics, is essential to understanding what your audience is interested in. This allows you to tailor your content accordingly and identify trends in your target market or local community. Social listening also aids in managing your online profiles and recognizing comments, complaints, or questions.

Paid Social Media Advertising: A Worthwhile Investment

Many Dental Practices are turning to paid ads on popular Social Media platforms. This shift is due to a decrease in organic content reach and an understanding of the power of targeted ads on these platforms. Paid advertisements on platforms like Instagram, Facebook, and LinkedIn can significantly increase your reach, engagement, and conversion rate.

Prior to spending on paid advertising with these platforms, make sure to develop your idea Patient Avatar. This will help you craft specific messaging, along with best understanding targeting, for the ideal types of patients you are looking to attract.

Developing a Winning Social Media Strategy

Creating an engaging social media strategy is all about planning, consistency, and interaction. Here's how to make it happen:

1. **Develop a Content Calendar:** This will help you plan and coordinate your posts across different platforms while maintaining a consistent posting schedule.

2. **Celebrate Special Days and Holidays:** Make the most of relevant observances like Dental Health Awareness Month, or even fun holidays like National Smile Day.

3. **Leverage User-Generated Content:** User-generated content such as patient testimonials or 'after-treatment' smile photos can significantly increase your credibility and authenticity.

4. **Engage with Your Audience:** Remember, Social Media is a two-way street. Responding to comments, answering queries, and hosting live sessions or webinars can dramatically boost your engagement.

5. **Collaborate with Other Local Businesses:** Cross-promotion or contests with local businesses can increase your visibility and reach on social media.

6. **Use Geo-targeting and Remarketing for Paid Ads:** Geo-targeting can help you reach people in your local area, while remarketing allows you to stay at the top of mind for people who've previously interacted with your brand.

7. **Experiment with A/B Testing:** This involves creating two different versions of an ad and tracking which one performs better. It's a great way to optimize your ads and improve results.

"Getting the Like is easy. It's a light action. Anything else requires trust."
- Jon Loomer

Social Media for Dentists isn't merely about gaining followers; it's about building trust, fostering relationships, and ultimately, expanding your practice. With the insights and strategies shared in this chapter, you're equipped to create engaging content, forge strong bonds with your audience, and transform your online presence. In the realm of social media, authenticity rules, engagement is the currency, and adaptability is the key to enduring success.

Getting more followers will be key, so here's some additional tips on how to do this!

1. Deliver Valuable Content

Content is king in the digital world. Ensure you consistently deliver valuable, engaging, and shareable content. Include informative posts about oral-health tips, behind-the-scenes glimpses of your practice, and patient testimonials. Also consider engaging elements like infographics, videos, and interactive quizzes.

2. Engage with Your Followers

Social Media is a two-way street. Be active and engage with your followers. Respond promptly to their comments and messages, ask for their opinions, and show appreciation for their interaction. Remember, every comment, like, and share increases your visibility.

3. Use Relevant Hashtags

Hashtags are a powerful tool for increasing your content's reach. Research and use relevant, popular hashtags in your posts. However, be careful not to overuse them—a handful of relevant hashtags often work better than a barrage of loosely connected ones.

4. Collaborate with Local Influencers

Influencer marketing is a powerful strategy. Collaborate with local influencers who resonate with your brand. Their endorsement can introduce your practice to a new audience and boost your credibility. Harnessing the power of influencer marketing can significantly impact your Dental Practice's outreach. By collaborating with local influencers who align with your brand's values and ethos, you open doors to vast audiences who trust and value their opinions.

Local influencers often have a dedicated follower base that places high trust in their recommendations. Their endorsement can significantly elevate your practice's credibility and visibility. When these influencers share their positive experiences with your practice, it's more than just a marketing message; it's a personal testimonial that carries weight.

Choosing the right influencer is a crucial part of this strategy. Look for influencers who have a genuine connection to their audience, exhibit a positive and healthy lifestyle, and, importantly, would be a good fit for your Dental Practice's philosophy. This could range from fitness trainers, local celebrities, to bloggers focused on health and lifestyle.

Additionally, consider the kind of collaboration that would best serve your practice. This might be an informative Q&A session about Dental health, a video showcasing a Dental procedure like teeth whitening, or even a candid testimonial following a Dental service. A well-executed influencer collaboration can provide authentic, relatable content that showcases your practice's services and commitment to patient care.

Influencer marketing, when executed correctly, offers a unique blend of reach, trust, and relevance. By leveraging local influencers, you can introduce your Dental Practice to a new demographic, elevate your credibility, and ultimately attract new patients. Remember, the goal is to create genuine, relatable content that resonates with the influencer's audience and aligns with your practice's values.

As always, remember to follow all HIPAA guidelines and any additional anti-kickback regulations that are necessary for your State when dealing with local influencers.

5. Use Paid Advertising

Consider using paid advertising to reach a wider audience. Platforms like Facebook and Instagram offer sophisticated targeting options, allowing your ads to reach the exact demographic you want to attract.

Growing your online following is not an overnight process—it requires consistent effort, patience, and adaptation. But with the right strategy and an authentic, patient-centered approach, you can cultivate a robust online community around your Dental Practice.

By telling compelling stories, engaging authentically with your followers, and providing value through your content, you'll not only increase your followers—you'll also deepen your connection with your online community.

"In the advertising din of today, unless you make yourself noticed and believed, you ain't got nothin'." ~ **Leo Burnett**

CHAPTER 19: HARNESSING THE POWER OF DENTAL CONTENT - FOSTERING STRONG BONDS WITH TEAMS AND PATIENTS

"The true measurement of any ad isn't the frequency of its appearance; it's the lasting impression it leaves."

~ Bill Bernbach

This chapter is dedicated to imparting invaluable guidance on generating dynamic, memorable content for your Dental Practice. In the realm of digital marketing, content indeed wears the crown. However, it's not just about the medium, whether video or written, but what your message conveys that leaves a lasting impression.

This doesn't imply that you can abandon the rules of grammar when drafting a caption or neglect to clean your phone's camera lens before recording. The emphasis is that your content's nature and its underlying message remain the paramount considerations.

Now, let's delve into the kind of content inspiration you've been eagerly anticipating.

Promote Patient Check-Ins

In the world of marketing, patient check-ins are the epitome of simplicity. When a patient checks in at your practice via social media, they inform their entire network of their location. Encouraging this practice is an excellent strategy to expand your word-of-mouth marketing organically. Implementing a simple sign in the reception area that prompts, "Check in and win a prize" is sufficient. Besides providing good publicity, check-ins also boost your organic SEO standing.

Ensure you have a genuine prize available. The prizes should be unique and personal, not run-of-the-mill like a generic gift certificate. Tailor them to reflect the personality of your Dental Practice or local flavor. Alternatively, if you're looking to attract transient patients, consider adding them to a raffle for a free cleaning. Always aim to offer something personal and unforgettable.

Gifts that leave an impression encourage patients to share their experiences, thereby promoting your practice to their friends and family. The crux of this check-in initiative is transforming your patients into ambassadors for your practice.

If you wish to infuse your marketing initiatives with altruism, consider donating a canned food item to a local food bank for every check-in. This charitable act fosters goodwill within the community. Always ensure the check-in prizes best represent the unique mission of your Dental Team.

Social Media Contests

Conducting regular social media contests promotes engagement, fun, and creativity across your platforms. Simple "Naming" or "Guessing" contests are recommended as they require minimal effort from your followers. Below are some innovative ideas:

Brushing Teddy Bear Contest: Utilize a Brushing Teddy Bear that plays an entertaining song for 2 minutes (the recommended brushing duration) while moving its toothbrush. Take a picture or video with your practice logo or reception area in the backdrop. Post this on social media, asking followers to name your new mascot. The most liked comment wins a prize like an Electric Toothbrush or another localized reward.

Floss Dispensers Contest: Fill a large glass vase or bowl with floss dispensers branded with your logo. Take a photo, post it on social media, and ask followers to guess the number of dispensers. The closest guess wins a personalized prize, possibly a restaurant gift certificate to the Dental Team's favorite local restaurant.

Travel, Brush, and Win Contest: Encourage your followers to share photos of themselves brushing their teeth in unique locations during their holidays. The Dental Team will vote on the most creative post, acknowledging all participants before announcing the winner and their prize. Ensure the prize personifies your practice elegantly.

While these are only a handful of potential social media contest ideas, countless other engaging activities could be integrated into your practice's unique personality and mission.

Please note, any and all prizes must be done randomly and not guaranteed. This helps ensure that you are complying with all HIPAA regulations and best practices for patient incentives.

"Good marketing makes the company look smart. Great marketing makes the customer feel smart."

~ Joe Chernov

Creating Your Content Library

When developing your content library, ensure it includes several formats to cater to different tastes and platforms. This section will discuss the types of content that elicit positive reactions and how to create a repertoire of unique content that performs exceptionally well across all platforms.

Education-Based Marketing: A timeless approach to marketing in Dental Practices, this involves informing patients about various Oral-Health topics through content marketing, reminding them subtly about your services. These "touches" refer to all marketing materials you publish both online and offline.

The main pointers in Education-Based Marketing are to educate rather than sell, and to concentrate on topics you wish to be known for. For instance, if your goal is to be recognized as a leading Dental Implants specialist, develop content around various Dental Implant topics. The content should address common queries about the topic while subtly informing them about your services.

For instance, we work with a Dental Office where hygienists are creating videos on topics like "Proper Tongue Cleaning," "Foods for Healthy Smiles," and "Effective Flossing Tips". These videos not only showcased the practice's unique character but also make their services more relatable and appealing. Capitalizing on Education-Based Marketing significantly enhances your branding, engagement, and conversion rates.

Content That Makes People Smile: Dental Marketing affords numerous opportunities for light-hearted, smile-inducing content. Quotes about smiles are especially shareable on social media platforms, and should be included regularly in your posts, reflecting your practice's unique branding style. This approach makes your content more appealing on social media feeds, leading to more sharing and engagement, fostering goodwill, and ultimately attracting new patients.

Developing an on-going content strategy and calendar will be so important for your success online, so make this part of your "Morning Huddles" or other regularly scheduled Team meetings. All of your Dental Team members, along with your head of marketing or agency, should be working together on a comprehensive plan to craft exceptional content together on a regular basis.

CHAPTER 20: INFUSING HUMOR AND HUMANITY IN YOUR DENTAL MARKETING CONTENT

"Laughter is the sun that drives winter from the human face."

- Victor Hugo

In an age where timelines are swamped with information, your Dental Practice can truly shine through the noise by weaving in humor and light-heartedness in your marketing messages. Embracing humor not only makes your content more engaging but also strengthens your brand's approachability and relatability.

As you embark on this journey, bear in mind that the humor incorporated should align with your Dental Practice's ethos, and exude elegance and class. If your Social Media content is being managed by a Team member or a marketing agency, establish guidelines together regarding the humor deemed appropriate. Striking the right balance can transform your content into a magnetic asset that aids your marketing efforts immensely.

While balancing education and entertainment in your content can be the golden ticket, it's important to identify which of the two resonates more with your target demographic. Whichever your practice leans towards, invest more energy into it while occasionally sprinkling the other. If your content is able to integrate both seamlessly, then you've truly hit a marketing home run!

Just for laughs, here's a few Dental jokes that could be implemented into your content initiatives:

1. Why did the smartphone go to the Dentist? Because it had a Bluetooth!
2. What do we call a Dentist who doesn't like tea? Denis!
3. What did the tooth say to the departing Dentist? Fill me in when you get back!
4. Why did the tree go to the Dentist? Because it needed a root canal!
5. What time do most people go to the Dentist? Tooth-hurty (2:30)!
6. Why don't Dentists seem scary? They have the power to 'extract' fear!
7. Why did the Dentist become a baseball coach? He knows the drill!
8. What did the molar say to the incisor? The Dentist is taking me out today!
9. Why did the king go to the Dentist? To get his teeth crowned!
10. What's a Dentist's favorite musical instrument? The tuba toothpaste!

Remember, humor is subjective, so it's essential to understand your audience and what they will find funny. These jokes should be used lightly and in good spirit as part of your Dental Practice's social media strategy. The goal is to engage, entertain, and create an uplifting association with your brand.

Consistency: The Bedrock of Social Media Presence

Social Media content thrives on consistency. Just like brushing your teeth, updating your Social Media profiles should be a regular activity. You can set recurring themes for specific days, such as 'Motivational Monday' posts or a Dental humor segment every Friday. The idea is to have content that is both relevant to Dentistry and engaging for your audience. For example, "Effort is like toothpaste. You can always squeeze out just a little bit more."

Creating a monthly content calendar can significantly streamline your posting schedule and help maintain a balanced frequency. It aids in ensuring that you are neither overwhelming nor under-serving your audience with content. Remember, the two pillars of a successful digital content strategy are creating captivating content and doing it consistently.

As for the frequency, aim to engage with your Social Media profiles daily. The nature of your posts could vary - from new technology introduced in your office, to training programs your team has completed, to awards your practice has bagged. The objective is to create a connection between these achievements and how they enhance patient treatment.

Take, for instance, if your practice recently transitioned to an intra-oral scanner, eliminating the need for traditional Dental impressions. Sharing this news would be a hit amongst your patients. The world's leading brands share a common trait: their phenomenal content touches various platforms consistently.

In today's dynamic digital landscape, popular influencers and brands churn out hundreds of content pieces weekly. While they may have a Team dedicated to content creation, the lesson here is clear - the more quality content, the better it is for your brand building.

So, based on what fits your Dental Team, your office, and your target demographic, ensure you're scheduling creative content regularly. By doing so, you'll witness enhanced fun, increased engagement, and most importantly, greater marketing success.

Engagement: The Social Media Success Mantra

Regardless of which Social Media platforms your Dental Practice prefers, proactive engagement is the key to success. It's crucial to ask questions and promptly respond to comments, posts, mentions, or messages. This responsiveness enhances your online reputation and fosters stronger connections with your audience.

Engagement isn't just about asking questions; it's also about appreciating the responses, acknowledging the participants, and sparking conversations. When someone recommends their favorite sushi spot in the city, make an effort to visit that place with your Dental Team. Post a picture of your team enjoying their sushi, tag the restaurant, and mention the person who recommended it. This approach creates local engagement, fosters community bonding, and opens doors for new patients.

Often, comments or queries related to insurance or oral health concerns get overlooked. Paying close attention to these and addressing them diligently is paramount. Each interaction is an opportunity to engage, just as you would engage in a friendly conversation in person.

Remember, your engagement efforts are a significant factor in increasing your organic reach, fostering community goodwill, and most importantly, acquiring new Dental Patients.

Celebrating Fun Holidays: The Perfect Recipe for Engagement

With a multitude of fun holidays scattered throughout the year, your Dental Office has ample opportunities for creative celebrations and posts. From seemingly random celebrations like National Guacamole Day or National Clean Your Floors Day, to more relevant ones like National Smile Day or Children's Dental Health Month, there is always a reason to celebrate.

For instance, on National Cheese Pizza Day, order some pizzas from a local pizzeria and share pictures of your team enjoying the meal. While tagging the pizzeria, share a Dental tip like, "If you're celebrating National Cheese Pizza Day today too, make sure to brush and floss your teeth thoroughly after enjoying food with dairy." Such posts demonstrate personality, offer value, and encourage engagement without overtly selling Dentistry.

Our DentalYear Mobile App simplifies this further by providing you with daily fun holiday ideas. By regularly celebrating these holidays, your practice will not only become a buzz in town but also ensure regular reach, engagement, and conversion.

The Audience of 1: Crafting Personalized Content

When creating your content, visualize the ideal person who would consume it. Is it a CEO looking for All-On-Dental Implants procedure? Or a parent searching for a Pediatric Dental office? Understanding your target audience's characteristics, preferences, and behavior allows you to craft content that resonates with them and compels them to take action.

This strategy, coupled with targeted ads on Social Media, ensures that your message is not just well-received but also acted upon. Remember, "A warm smile is the universal language of kindness." - William Arthur Ward. So, let your marketing content radiate the warmth and kindness that your practice stands for, one smile at a time.

What are the ideal times to post on Social Media? We'll here's some insights into the best practices:

Posting when your audience is most active can significantly enhance the reach and engagement of your content. However, it's essential to note that the "best" time to post can vary based on factors like your specific audience, their online habits, and the social media platform you're using. Here's a general guide to the ideal times to post on various social media platforms:

1. Facebook

Typically, the best times to post on Facebook are between 9 am and 2 pm during weekdays, with peak engagement occurring on Wednesday. However, given the diversity of users on Facebook, these times may vary based on your specific audience. Make use of Facebook Insights to understand when your followers are most active.

2. Instagram

For Instagram, weekdays often yield the best engagement, specifically Monday, Wednesday, and Thursday. The ideal times are usually around lunch (11 am to 1 pm) and in the evening (7 pm to 9 pm). Instagram Insights is a valuable tool for gaining a deeper understanding of your audience's online behavior.

3. Twitter

Twitter sees consistent engagement from Monday to Friday, with peak times often between 8 am and 4 pm. This platform tends to be more active during work hours. As with other platforms, utilize Twitter Analytics to gain insight into your specific followers' habits.

4. LinkedIn

Given its professional focus, LinkedIn sees the highest engagement during work hours, with Tuesday, Wednesday, and Thursday being the most active days. The best times to post tend to be at the start and end of the workday (around 7-8:30 AM and 5-6 PM).

5. Pinterest

Pinterest users tend to be most active in the evening and on weekends, with Saturday and Sunday evenings proving particularly fruitful.

Remember, these are broad guidelines and might not perfectly apply to your unique audience. The key to mastering the timing of social media posts is understanding your audience and their habits. Make use of the analytics tools provided by each platform and be prepared to test different posting times to see what yields the best results for your Dental Practice.

Furthermore, keep in mind that quality always trumps quantity. It's better to post less frequently and offer high-value content than to post constantly with content that doesn't engage your audience. As Peter Drucker, a well-respected management consultant, once said, "There is nothing so useless as doing efficiently that which should not be done at all." Make sure your social media efforts align with your overall marketing strategy and resonate with your audience—that's the real key to social media success.

CHAPTER 21: REVOLUTIONIZING DENTAL PRACTICE MARKETING WITH ARTIFICIAL INTELLIGENCE - KEY PRINCIPLES AND EFFECTIVE STRATEGIES

"The complexity of simplicity cannot be overstated."
~ Leonardo Da Vinci

Understanding the Role of AI in Dental Practice Marketing

Artificial intelligence (AI) is not just an emerging trend, it has established itself as a game-changer across a myriad of industries, and the realm of Dentistry is no different. AI possesses transformative power, capable of redefining how Dental Practices understand, engage, and serve their patients. In addition, it enhances the efficiency and efficacy of various internal workflows. This chapter aims to shed light on the myriad ways AI can be leveraged in Dental Marketing, and how it can significantly boost a Dental Practice's performance and profitability.

One of the principal advantages of AI in Dental Marketing lies in its capacity to personalize patient communication. Sophisticated AI algorithms can delve into patient data, crafting customized marketing initiatives that speak to their unique requirements and preferences. The outcome is elevated engagement and conversion rates, as patients feel recognized, understood, and valued.

Another significant domain where AI can add substantial value in Dental Marketing is via chatbots. These AI-empowered virtual assistants can handle rudimentary patient inquiries and facilitate appointment scheduling, liberating staff time for more intricate tasks. Furthermore, chatbots can be instrumental in gathering patient feedback and offering personalized treatment suggestions.

AI's applications aren't restricted to direct patient communication. It's also a powerful tool for refining a Dental Practice's online presence. By examining patient data, AI algorithms can detect patterns and trends that can be harnessed to enhance the layout, design, and content of a practice's website and social media platforms. The result? Enhanced visibility, elevated engagement, and an influx of prospective patient leads.

Beyond these applications, AI can drive significant improvements in internal processes like appointment scheduling, billing, and patient management. AI-driven appointment scheduling software can intelligently pair patients with suitable appointment slots, minimizing missed appointments. Similarly, AI-powered billing software can process and reconcile payments autonomously, lightening the staff's workload.

Ultimately, AI possesses the potential to radically alter the marketing and operational approaches of Dental Practices. By harnessing AI's power, Dental Practices can deepen their understanding of and connection with patients, while simultaneously refining and optimizing diverse internal procedures.

However, it's crucial to remember that every technology comes with its potential risks and limitations, and AI is no different. Considerations around data privacy, job displacement, and ethical concerns must not be overlooked. It's equally important to ensure that AI applications in use adhere to principles of fairness and transparency.

In conclusion, AI emerges as a formidable asset that can aid Dental Practices in amplifying their marketing strategies, patient engagement, and internal operations. By comprehending and harnessing AI's capabilities,

Dental Practices can stay competitive, future-proof their operations, and enhance their chances of success.

Pioneering a New Era in Dental Marketing: AI Adoption

If your Dental Marketing initiatives are not yielding the desired outcomes, it's time to reconsider your approach. More precisely, you might be executing things flawlessly, but there's room for expansion and enhancement using more contemporary strategies like artificial intelligence (AI) marketing.

AI technology, since its advent, has evolved dramatically. Today, it offers capabilities that, in some cases, surpass human capabilities. An illustrative example is ChatGPT by OpenAI, a language model that poses a legitimate challenge to Google's search predominance.

Though AI isn't about to conquer the world, it is poised to significantly enhance productivity and efficiency within your Dental Practice. It also promises remarkable improvement in your return on investment (ROI). Here are a few notable examples of recent AI applications: Google's RankBrain, Air BnB's Algorithm Pricing, Dell's Automated Emails, Google's Voice Search, and Hemingway for Editing.

These examples represent only the tip of the AI iceberg. An increasing number of Dental Practices, both large and small, are integrating AI into their comprehensive marketing strategies. Let's delve deeper into some of the specific ways you can weave AI into your digital and traditional Dental marketing methods.

Content Creation & Generation with AI

While AI may not yet be able to pen an opinion piece or compose an insightful blog post, it possesses some compelling capabilities that can drive traffic to your website.

Consider this: AI is currently able to generate news articles and reports based on supplied information and data. Tools such as Articoolo, Quill, and Wordsmith have facilitated news writing for notable companies such as Forbes and Associated Press. The AI-generated articles foster increased website traffic.

How does this magic happen? Templates guide the process as you input keywords and data. While we're simplifying the process, the AI system then aids in producing original content that's indistinguishable from human-written content. You likely encounter AI-created content daily without even realizing it. If you've engaged with content produced by Reuters, the New York Times, CBS, or the BBC, you've interacted with AI-assisted writing.

Content Curation for Dental Marketing with AI

AI's capabilities extend beyond content creation. It can also significantly improve your user experience by consistently engaging visitors. AI technology commonly powers personalized recommendations, enhancing user engagement. Imagine the potential impact if your Dental Practice site could provide statements such as, "patients who tried this also had this procedure." This could lead to increased website retention, making your website more sticky.

Linking relevant articles in your blog also contributes to effective content curation. Interlinking is a proven method for retaining visitors on your website.

Marketing with Email & AI for Dental Practices

Dental Practices can leverage AI to personalize email campaigns. With the assistance of machine learning, your practice can delve into data about your current and potential patients, identifying optimal times to make contact.

Digital Advertising with AI

Digital marketing has reaped considerable benefits from AI. Platforms like Google and Facebook Ads use AI and machine learning to understand what triggers a user to engage with a post. By analyzing likes, dislikes, demographics, and interests, the algorithms can better serve users.

When digital marketing is integrated with traditional marketing techniques, like including a QR code on postcards, your reach expands to a broader audience - potentially attracting new patients.

"Personalization — it is not about first/last name. It's about relevant content."

~ Dan Jak

Harnessing artificial intelligence (AI) to supercharge your marketing endeavors is an opportunity that cannot be overlooked. The tools and techniques outlined above can streamline and enhance your content curation and generation, as well as content distribution processes. With a balanced focus on digital marketing and traditional marketing techniques, you can embrace the future while respecting the past. This will keep your Dental Practice competitive, innovative, and successful for years to come.

CHAPTER 22: UNLEASHING THE POWER OF CHATGPT IN DENTAL MARKETING - INSIGHTS, EXAMPLES, AND SUCCESS STORIES

"AI doesn't replace the dentist; it amplifies their capabilities."

~ Anonymous

Delving Deeper into ChatGPT

ChatGPT, a transformative creation by OpenAI, stands tall as a prominent model of how artificial intelligence is revolutionizing digital communication. At its core, ChatGPT is a conversational AI system, trained using a dataset comprising parts of the internet, making it an incredibly dynamic and versatile tool.

While some view the growing AI trend with skepticism, considering it to be a potential threat to human employment, it's important to remember the profound words of Kevin Kelly: "You'll be paid in the future based on how well you work with robots." Instead of replacing humans, AI systems like ChatGPT act as powerful tools that augment our capabilities, making us more productive and efficient.

Applying ChatGPT in Dental Marketing: Real-World Examples

Let's take a look at some compelling examples of how Dental practices can incorporate ChatGPT into their marketing strategies, transforming the way they interact with current and prospective patients.

1. Virtual Receptionist: ChatGPT can act as a virtual receptionist for your Dental Practice, available 24/7 to interact with website visitors. It can answer basic queries about your services, operating hours, or appointment availability, offering immediate responses that can be pivotal in capturing and converting leads.

2. Appointment Scheduling: In a seamless and efficient manner, ChatGPT can manage appointment scheduling. By interacting with patients, it can identify suitable slots, book appointments, and even send reminders, minimizing no-shows.

3. Feedback Collection: ChatGPT can engage with patients post-treatment to gather valuable feedback. By analyzing this data, you can gain insights into patient satisfaction, areas of improvement, and even success stories for your marketing content.

4. Treatment Recommendations: Based on the patients' reported symptoms or concerns, ChatGPT can suggest potential treatment options, acting as an informative resource. While it's not a substitute for professional Dental consultation, it can provide patients with an initial understanding, setting the stage for further professional interaction.

5. Personalized Marketing: ChatGPT can enhance your email marketing efforts by crafting personalized emails. These could range from appointment reminders and promotional offers to educational content tailored to each patient's unique Dental Health history and needs.

"Innovation needs to be part of your culture. Consumers are transforming faster than we are, and if we don't catch up, we're in trouble."

- Ian Schafer

Success Stories: ChatGPT in Action

To illustrate the transformative impact of ChatGPT in Dental Marketing, let's delve into a few success stories:

1. **Optimized Scheduling:** A Boston-based Dental Practice employed ChatGPT to handle their appointment scheduling process. The AI tool interacted with patients in real-time to book appointments, resulting in a significant reduction in no-shows and an impressive increase in the number of appointments scheduled after hours.

2. **Enhanced Customer Service:** A Dental Practice in northern California leveraged ChatGPT to answer queries on their website. This resulted in an increase in website engagement, with prospective patients spending more time on the site, leading to a substantial rise in appointment bookings.

3. **Personalized Marketing:** A small town Dental Clinic decided to integrate ChatGPT into their email marketing strategy. The AI tool sent personalized emails to the clinic's patients based on their individual needs and Dental history, resulting in a notable increase in patient engagement and conversion rates.

4. **Video Creativity:** A Pacific Northwest Dental Practice started to produce regular video content that has engaged, inspired and educated their followers on a variety of oral-health topics and advanced Dental technology capabilities.

5. **Online Course:** A reputable and world renown clinician helped personalize their online course for users in different languages, thus allowing them to reach and impact many more people.

These are just a few examples demonstrating how ChatGPT can revolutionize Dental Marketing. By adopting this AI-powered tool, Dental

Practices can engage with their patients in a more personalized and efficient manner, thereby enhancing their marketing outcomes and the overall patient experience.

"AI is not meant to replace humans but to enhance human capabilities and simplify tasks."

~ Dr. Marc Teerlink

A 2023 Mailchimp survey found that half of the marketers believed their marketing goals were hampered by inadequate AI adoption. Further, an overwhelming 88% felt that increased usage of AI and automation is essential for meeting customer expectations and maintaining competitiveness in their respective industries.

This sentiment resonates with marketers as well. According to the recent Influencer Marketing Hub's report, more than half (54.5%) anticipate that AI will significantly enhance their marketing efforts. More astonishingly, a substantial 71.2% believe AI has the potential to outperform humans at their jobs.

Additionally, 61.4% of marketers have already integrated AI into their marketing activities. AI's potential in content production is also being recognized, with 44.4% of marketers leveraging it for this purpose. The commitment to AI-driven campaigns is further evident in budget allocations, with 19.2% of marketers investing more than 40% of their budget in AI-centric campaigns.

These statistics illustrate a growing acknowledgment of AI's transformative power in marketing. Embracing AI and automation can equip your Dental Practice with powerful tools to understand and connect with your audience, deliver personalized experiences, optimize your marketing efforts, and ultimately, drive growth.

As we venture further into the era of AI, Dental Practices must seize this opportunity to enhance themselves. As technology futurist Daniel Burrus wisely stated, "An anticipatory leader is one who sees a game-changing opportunity that others don't and moves swiftly to capitalize on it." In the realm of Dental Marketing, AI presents such a game-changing opportunity—do not just keep up with the times, anticipate and shape the future.

As we continue to harness the potential of AI technologies like ChatGPT, the future of Dental Marketing seems poised to be one of amplified human potential, greater operational efficiency, and enhanced patient satisfaction. A future where AI and human ingenuity coexist, creating a Dental healthcare experience that's seamless, personalized, and above all, patient-centric.

CHAPTER 23: HARNESSING THE POWER OF REVIEWS FOR DENTAL PRACTICE SUCCESS - A DEEP DIVE INTO STRATEGIES, IMPACT, AND BEST PRACTICES

"Your brand isn't what you say it is. It's what Google says it is."

~ Chris Anderson, Former Editor of Wired Magazine

Embracing the Influence of Reviews in Dental Practices

In our hyperconnected age, online reviews act as a digital currency of trust and reputation. The importance they carry in the realm of Dental Practices is analogous to personal recommendations, making them an integral part of a practice's online footprint.

A compelling statistic from BrightLocal sets the stage: 85% of consumers value online reviews as highly as personal recommendations. This statistic paints a vivid picture of the impact online reviews have for Dental Practices. They serve as a key litmus test, providing prospective patients with a window into the patient experience at your office.

Positive reviews shine a spotlight on your practice, guiding potential patients to your services in a highly competitive landscape. They amplify your practice's reputation, foster patient loyalty, and draw in new patients. In stark contrast, negative reviews can cast a pall, potentially turning away prospective patients.

Proactive Management and Thoughtful Responses: Navigating the Sea of Reviews

The principle 'Prevention is better than cure' rings as true for managing your online reputation as it does for oral health. Proactive monitoring of online reviews equips you to address issues promptly, safeguarding your practice's reputation.

Setting up alerts for new reviews and regularly checking review websites and social media platforms can give you a clear perspective on patient sentiment. Responding to negative reviews is a delicate balance of diplomacy and sincerity. A professional demeanor, empathetic apologies, and tangible solutions can help mitigate the impact of negative reviews and signal your dedication to patient satisfaction.

Engaging with positive reviews is equally crucial. Expressing gratitude for a patient's feedback not only reinforces loyalty but also demonstrates your appreciation for their effort. It sends a powerful message: You value your patients and their experiences.

Cultivating Reviews: Fostering a Feedback-First Culture

Encouraging patients to leave reviews can significantly enhance your online visibility. Two key strategies stand out in this regard: Direct solicitation and incentives.

Direct Solicitation: Offering patients a card or email with a link to a review website or your practice's social media page post-appointment can be very effective. Reminding patients that their feedback is instrumental in enhancing your services also motivates them to share their experiences.

Incentives: Providing incentives such as future service discounts or contest entries can stimulate patients to leave a review. However, it's paramount to ensure HIPAA compliance with the terms of service of the relevant review websites or social media platforms.

Randomized incentives are way more appropriate than guaranteed ones, as these usually fall within the scope of approval for HIPAA purposes. Although, always make sure to check on the best practices in your particular state.

"Character is like a tree and reputation is like its shadow. The shadow is what we think of it; the tree is the real thing."

~ Abraham Lincoln

Charting the Path to Success: Leveraging Reviews for Dental Practice Growth

Online reviews form a critical component of a Dental Practice's online persona and overall reputation. By diligently managing and responding to reviews, Dental Offices can cultivate a positive image, thereby attracting new patients and bolstering patient loyalty.

Promoting a culture that values and solicits patient feedback allows practices to gain valuable insights to continually refine and enhance their services. Tapping into the power of reviews in this manner can ignite growth, setting Dental Practices apart in a crowded marketplace, and creating a platform for unmatched patient experiences.

Leveraging the influence of reviews, Dental Practices can unlock a potent tool for their marketing arsenal, bolstering their reputation and enhancing their patient relationships. Besides Google reviews, make sure to also focus on those Video Patient Testimonials we covered earlier in this book. Video is an absolute game-changer and without question the most powerful form of mult-media content.

CHAPTER 24: NAVIGATING THE CROSSROADS OF TRADITIONAL AND DIGITAL MARKETING TO ENSURE DENTAL PRACTICE SUCCESS

"Make the customer the hero of your story."

~ Ann Handley, Marketing Prose

Setting the Stage: Understanding the Marketing Landscape in Dentistry

While Dentistry can be seen as a niche market, the underpinning requirement for success in this industry transcends this categorization. At the heart of a thriving Dental Practice is a robust and continually evolving marketing strategy encompassing both traditional and digital elements. This strategic blend ensures a steady stream of new patients, bolstering the practice's growth trajectory and longevity. In this fast-paced, ever-evolving business landscape, marketing strategies must not only resonate with the audience but also stand out as fresh and unique.

Bearing the brunt of crafting innovative marketing plans can be an intimidating challenge. This chapter aims to demystify the interplay of traditional and digital marketing in the Dental industry, offering insights to help you steer your marketing ship successfully.

Contrasting Worlds: Traditional vs. Digital Marketing

One question we often encounter is the differentiation between traditional and digital marketing, and the relevance of the former in this digitally dominated era. Our perspective: Every marketing tool carries inherent value, and can be skillfully adapted to engage contemporary audiences. Let's delve deeper into this dichotomy.

Traditional marketing refers to time-tested methods such as television and radio ads, billboards, direct mail, and print media. Despite the rise of digital platforms, these channels continue to hold sway, particularly among certain demographics and local markets. Their tactile nature, broad reach, and perceived trustworthiness make them a potent component of a holistic marketing strategy.

On the flip side, digital marketing leverages online channels and technology to engage with consumers. This includes techniques such as search engine optimization (SEO), social media marketing, email marketing, and content marketing. The greatest advantages of digital marketing lie in its targeted reach, personalization capabilities, real-time performance tracking, and cost-effectiveness. With the pervasive influence of the internet in our lives, digital marketing has become a cornerstone for businesses to connect with the modern consumer.

The Marriage of Traditional and Digital: A Paradigm Shift in Dental Practice Marketing

While traditional and digital marketing may appear as polar opposites, their synergy can create a marketing strategy that is greater than the sum of its parts. The trick lies in understanding the strengths of each approach and cleverly integrating them to maximize their combined potential.

For instance, a direct mail campaign (traditional marketing) could be coupled with a personalized follow-up email campaign (digital marketing). A billboard ad could carry a QR code, bridging the offline-online gap and driving traffic to your website or social media platform. A TV or radio ad could promote an online contest or discount code, prompting audiences to engage with your digital channels.

In Dentistry, a well-rounded marketing strategy could look like this: Billboards and print media ads raise brand awareness in local communities. A compelling website optimized for local SEO draws in those seeking Dental services online. Social Media channels facilitate patient engagement, testimonials, and reviews, enhancing online reputation. Regularly emailed newsletters keep patients updated on the latest services, offers, or oral health tips, fostering a sense of community.

Creating and implementing such a cohesive marketing strategy, however, requires deep understanding, creativity, and constant evolution in response to changing trends and customer behavior.

Navigating Forward: The Future of Marketing in Dental Practices

In this digital age, where even our toothbrushes have become smart, marketing for Dental Practices requires more than just a one-size-fits-all approach. It's about marrying the best of traditional and digital marketing strategies to create a customized, multi-channel strategy that speaks to your target audience. By doing so, not only will you attract and retain more patients, but you will also cement your Dental Practice's position as a trusted, forward-thinking, patient-centric entity.

CHAPTER 25: LEVERAGING THE POWER OF DUAL MARKETING - TRADITIONAL AND DIGITAL MARKETING STRATEGIES PRACTICE GROWTH

"Adaptability is the simple secret of survival."

~ Jessica Hagedorn, Writer and Poet

Change is the only constant in life, and this adage holds true in the realm of marketing as well. The advent of digital technology has indeed revolutionized the way we market our businesses. But it hasn't annihilated the relevance of traditional marketing. Instead, it has prompted a transformation, a metamorphosis that equips traditional marketing strategies with new wings to soar in today's climate. The key to success, therefore, lies in crafting a marketing approach that elegantly merges the traditional with the digital.

Traditional Marketing: The Immortal Classic

While traditional marketing may appear somewhat aged compared to its digital counterpart, it retains a strong foothold in the marketing world. Its tools and methods continue to play a crucial role in branding and promotion. The mainstays of traditional marketing include:

- Direct mail
- Magazines
- Newspapers
- Radio/TV

- Billboards
- Taxi/Bus Wraps
- Roadside Signage
- Telemarketing
- Window Displays
- Outdoor/Indoor Signage

In the context of Dental Marketing, these tools can be highly effective. For example, an attractive billboard in a strategic location or a well-crafted TV ad can significantly elevate brand visibility. However, the trick lies in ensuring that these traditional tactics are up-to-date and resonate with today's audience.

Digital Marketing: The Contemporary Powerhouse

Though a relative newcomer, digital marketing has swiftly taken the center stage. It offers a more personalized, interactive, and measurable approach to reaching out to potential patients. Digital marketing tools include:

- Email
- Social Media Marketing
- Voice Search Marketing
- Online Marketing
- Text Marketing
- Chatbots
- Content Marketing
- Video Production
- Pay Per Click
- SEO
- AI Marketing

Digital marketing opens a plethora of opportunities for Dental Practices. From enhancing online visibility with SEO to building patient relationships through social media, digital tools offer multi-dimensional pathways to marketing success.

The Fusion of Traditional and Digital: The Hybrid Strategy

While both traditional and digital marketing have their strengths, blending them into a hybrid strategy amplifies their impact. This fusion ensures a wider reach, higher engagement, and a more holistic approach. But how does one go about combining these two seemingly distinct strategies? Here are some ideas:

1. Integrated Campaigns: Launch marketing campaigns that use both traditional and digital channels. For instance, a TV ad (traditional) can prompt viewers to visit a landing page (digital) for more information or special offers.

2. QR Codes: Use QR codes on print media ads, billboards, or direct mail to bridge the gap between offline and online realms. Scanning these codes can take potential patients directly to your website, social media page, or promotional video.

3. Social Media Teasers: Create buzz around your upcoming print media ad or TV commercial by posting teasers on your social media channels. This strategy creates a loop that encourages engagement on multiple platforms.

4. Email and Direct Mail: Combine email and direct mail campaigns. An email newsletter could be followed by a personalized direct mail piece, reinforcing your message and increasing the chances of engagement.

In essence, achieving a harmonious blend of traditional and digital marketing hinges on creativity, innovation, and a thorough understanding of your target audience. As Marshall McLuhan, a renowned media theorist, once said, "The medium is the message." To captivate your audience effectively, the message (your marketing content) and the medium (traditional or digital channel) must harmonize, creating a symphony that resounds in the heart of your audience. By crafting such a hybrid marketing strategy, Dental Practices can enjoy the best of both worlds, yielding a greater ROI and a richer patient relationship.

CHAPTER 26: HARNESSING THE POTENTIAL OF PRINT MEDIA AND DEEP MEDIA NURTURING

"The aim of marketing is to know and understand the customer so well the product or service fits him and sells itself."

~ Peter F. Drucker

In an era where digital marketing often steals the limelight, the potential of print media and deep media nurturing is often overlooked. However, the true power of marketing lies in blending both traditional and digital platforms to create a holistic strategy that leaves no stone unturned.

The Dual Facets of Media Nurturing

The objective of deep media nurturing, along with print media, is to draw as much attention as possible using every accessible channel. This multi-pronged approach enhances the likelihood of customer conversion. While print media may not hold center stage as it once did, publications like magazines and newspapers still command a sizeable audience.

Print media, by nature, is subtler than digital ads. Its less intrusive approach provides more flexibility for Dental advertisement placement. In contrast to the bidding wars of programmatic display advertising for online newspaper ad placements, print media offers more control over where your ad is placed.

Capitalizing on Geotargeting

Geotargeting - reaching out to potential customers based on their geographical location - is a potent tool in the marketer's arsenal. Electronic billboards offer an excellent medium for geo-targeting your ads, giving prospective patients in your locality the opportunity to visit your Dental Practice.

When you pair the power of digital ads and billboards with geotargeting, you not only drive brand awareness but also emphasize your identity as a local Dental practitioner. Outdoor signage and billboards, strategically placed to attract local residents, can significantly boost your local presence.

Marrying Email and Direct Mail

Merging email and direct mail marketing can be a delicate dance. People's inbox settings often filter unknown senders into the spam folder. To circumvent this, careful crafting of email blasts is required, with each email offering something of value to the recipient. Personalization of email blasts, including relevant patient data or social media activity, enhances engagement. Including a short video clip in the email teaser can significantly boost open rates, as research suggests people are more likely to open emails with embedded videos.

Power of Personalization

No matter how you choose to advertise your Dental Practice, personalization remains the key. Every interaction, from social media engagement to postcards and in-office marketing, must be designed to personally engage every inquiry. Make sure to obsess about personalization across all marketing channels, as this alone will help increase conversions and lower the overall cost of acquiring each new patient.

Elevating Email Marketing

As a Dental Practice, building relationships with your patients is paramount. Email marketing is a potent tool for forging these relationships, promoting your practice, and encouraging patients to schedule appointments. Some best practices for leveraging email marketing are:

1. Building an email list
2. Personalizing emails
3. Using a professional email marketing service
4. Segmenting your email list
5. Crafting a clear subject line
6. Keeping the email brief
7. Including a Call-To-Action
8. Testing and optimizing your campaigns

Tradition Meets Modernity

By embracing both traditional and digital advertising, you ensure comprehensive coverage, appealing to both online-savvy customers and those who prefer traditional methods. The amalgamation of geotargeted billboards and social media marketing enables you to reach audiences you might have otherwise missed.

The essence of it all is to blend your efforts with effective ideas that contribute to your Dental practice's growth. As Ben Grossman wisely said, "New marketing is about relationships, not the medium." It's about finding what works best for you, updating traditional marketing to modern standards, and constantly pushing the boundaries of your current marketing strategies. A dynamic, flexible approach to marketing can set your Dental Practice apart in the competitive healthcare landscape.

CHAPTER 27: UNLEASHING THE POTENTIAL OF YOUR DENTAL TEAM - THE ART OF EMPOWERMENT

"Coming together is a beginning, staying together is progress, and working together is success."

- Henry Ford

The journey of transformation begins with empowerment, an act that fuels morale, cultivates an inviting environment, and encourages a drive for excellence within your Dental Team. Empowering your Team is an investment in your practice's future. It infuses your workspace with vitality and enthusiasm that your patients can sense and appreciate, creating a ripple effect that magnifies the quality of their experience. The key lies in distributing responsibility; when your Team members own specific tasks, they feel more motivated to excel, fostering a healthy competition that stimulates continuous improvement.

As James Clear points out in his insightful and highly recommended book, Atomic Habits, "Habits are the compound interest of self-improvement." By cultivating habits of empowerment within your Team, the incremental changes may seem minor day to day, but over time, the cumulative effects can be transformative.

A paramount area for employee empowerment is marketing. In our modern digital era, consumers extensively use social media and the internet for purchase decisions or booking appointments. Therefore, maintaining an active, engaging online presence is crucial. Here are three steps to empower your Dental Team in managing your online presence:

1. Appoint a Chief Marketing Officer: Have a dedicated person to lead your marketing strategies and manage your social media conversations.
2. Track Performance: Delegate another team member to monitor content effectiveness and measure ROI for marketing initiatives.
3. Reward Creativity: Encourage and reward team members who produce compelling content as it contributes significantly to your outreach efforts.

"Individual commitment to a group effort--that is what makes a team work, a company work, a society work, a civilization work."

- Vince Lombardi

Recognition of hard work is an effective morale booster that fosters Team spirit. It is essential to invest not only in your Team but also in yourself. Nurture your leadership skills and help your team members acquire new abilities. When your team thrives, so does your practice.

Engaging the Local Community

While maintaining a robust online presence is critical, as a Dental practitioner, your clientele interacts with you physically. Consequently, marketing within your community becomes a vital aspect of your promotional efforts, helping your practice garner attention and recognition.

The 8 x 10 Framed Picture Initiative

Start by identifying local businesses you appreciate. Perhaps a restaurant, a dry cleaner, or a car wash; places with pictures adorning their walls. Snap a warm, welcoming picture of your Dental Team, print it in an 8 x 10 size, and pen a heartfelt note appreciating the chosen business. For instance:

"Thanks so much for being our favorite sushi place in Boulder! Much love and appreciation, Boulder Dental Office."

Personalize this message to match the chosen business and your location. Hand-deliver this picture to the business manager or owner, expressing your gratitude for their service. The objective is to have them display your team's picture, introducing their patrons to your practice in an unexpected yet delightful manner.

Optimizing the Initial Interaction

The first impression is often the most lasting one. Usually, the first contact prospective patients have with your Dental practice is a phone call. It's paramount to exude an upbeat attitude from the get-go. Even a smile, invisible over the phone, can be sensed in the speaker's voice. Personalize the interaction by asking for the caller's name and use it throughout the conversation.

"Teamwork is the ability to work together toward a common vision. The ability to direct individual accomplishments toward organizational objectives. It is the fuel that allows common people to attain uncommon results."

- Andrew Carnegie

Ensure that your phone lines are always attended to, even during off-hours and lunch breaks. The aim is to always make the caller feel valued and acknowledged. Remember, every interaction with a prospective patient is an opportunity to create a positive, lasting impression and transform them into a long-term patient.

According to a recent report, nearly 85% of customers whose calls aren't answered will not call back, and an astonishing 75% of those callers will not leave a voicemail, emphasizing the importance of always having someone available to answer the phone. Moreover, a study by BT Business revealed that businesses could be losing out on as much as 20% of their potential customers due to missed calls.

In the context of a Dental Practice, these missed calls could equate to significant missed opportunities – potential new patients, appointments, or even referrals. With the Dental industry becoming increasingly competitive, it's crucial to prioritize prompt, professional, and courteous phone communication. Ensuring that your phone lines are always attended to is not just about good customer service; it's a strategic move that can directly impact your practice's growth and success. Remember, every call is an opportunity, and every opportunity counts in building and maintaining a thriving Dental Practice.

Removing any friction and capturing these "micro-moments" with new patients is such an important aspect of everyone's marketing success. As a Dental Team, make sure these aspects of your office are dialed-in and fully optimized for conversions.

CHAPTER 28: CULTIVATING YOUR DENTAL BRAND - THE ESSENCE OF AUTHENTICITY

"Be yourself - everyone else is already taken."

- Oscar Wilde

The concept of branding goes far beyond a logo or a catchy slogan. In essence, it's the emotional and psychological relationship you establish with your patients. It's a fundamental element that sets your Dental Practice apart from the crowd and communicates your unique value proposition. Your brand is the essence of your practice's identity, an embodiment of the values you uphold and the promises you make to your patients.

Imagine walking down the beverage aisle of a supermarket. You see a distinctly shaped soda bottle filled with a familiar dark liquid and adorned with a red wrap sticker. Your mind instantly recognizes it as Coca-Cola. Similarly, particular shades of brown might remind you of UPS, and certain blues evoke the luxury of Tiffany & Co. This immediate recognition is the power of effective branding, which, although might seem exclusive to mega-brands, is equally essential for a Dental Practice.

In the realm of Dentistry, your brand identity should be an amalgamation of your professional competence, exceptional patient care, empathetic communication, and a warm, inviting environment. It should resonate with your target audience and compel them to choose you over competitors in the local community. Once you do this properly, all aspects of your marketing strategy will soar to new heights.

"Your brand is a story unfolding across all customer touch points."

- Jonah Sachs

Branding is not a one-time affair; rather, it's an ongoing narrative that unfolds at every patient touchpoint, from the first phone call to the follow-up post-treatment. Each interaction is a golden opportunity to reinforce your brand values, instill confidence in your patients, and build lasting relationships. A consistent, memorable brand experience can turn first-time patients into loyal ones and amplify word-of-mouth referrals.

Here are a few pointers to consider while cultivating your Dental brand:

1. Define Your Unique Selling Proposition (USP): Understand what sets your Dental practice apart from competitors. Is it the latest technology you employ, your exceptional patient care, or your unparalleled expertise in a particular Dental procedure? Once you have identified your USP, incorporate it into your branding strategy.

2. Create a Memorable Logo and Tagline: Your logo is the face of your brand, and your tagline is its voice. Both should be simple, engaging, and reflective of your USP.

3. Website and Online Presence: In the digital age, your website serves as your virtual office. Ensure it aligns with your brand image, offers a user-friendly experience, and provides comprehensive information about your services. Regularly update your social media channels to engage with your audience and reinforce your brand identity.

4. Consistent Communication: Ensure your brand's voice is consistent across all touchpoints, be it your website content, social media posts, newsletters, or patient interactions. Consistency strengthens brand recognition and builds patient trust.

5. Team Training: Your entire Team should understand and reflect your brand values. Train them to communicate effectively, maintain an upbeat demeanor, and provide top-notch patient care, all of which contribute to a consistent brand experience.

6. Patient Experience: Beyond excellent Dental care, focus on enhancing the overall patient experience. From a comfortable waiting area to post-treatment follow-ups, every little detail matters. Happy patients are the best ambassadors for your brand, as they will generate referrals and goodwill for years to come.

True authenticity is vital to a successful brand. If your brand appears extensively on social media but lacks a tangible presence in the local community, there's a disconnect that needs to be addressed. Remember, your practice isn't an isolated entity; it's an integral part of your local community. It's where your patients live, shop, and work. Ensuring a prominent community presence and empowering your team to represent your brand can result in significant benefits. This balance between online and offline branding efforts, coupled with a consistent, authentic brand story, will create a magnetic effect that draws patients to your practice.

Besides always trying to be opportunistic for marketing opportunities, always be open to ways in which you can give back and benefit your local community without ever expecting anything in return.

"Our culture is built around the idea of giving back and making the world a better place."

- Marc Benioff

CHAPTER 29: CRAFTING THE IDEAL LOGO - ARTICULATING YOUR DENTAL BRAND

"Logos and branding are so important. In a big part of the world, people cannot read French or English--but are great in remembering signs."

- Karl Lagerfeld

A Guide to Logo Design

Your logo is an extension of your Dental brand. It's more than an attractive graphic; it's a symbolic representation of your practice's ethos, values, and services. As you embark on the process of designing your logo, it's useful to draw inspiration from the logos of well-known brands that have effectively conveyed their messages. Let's take a look at a few examples:

- **FedEx:** The FedEx logo is renowned for its hidden design element. At first glance, it appears to be simple typography, but a closer look between the 'E' and 'x' reveals an arrow. This forward-pointing arrow represents speed, precision, and forward-looking nature of the company. Despite its simplicity, the FedEx logo communicates a lot about the company's values and services. It's a great example of the power of hidden or negative space in design.

- **Starbucks:** The Starbucks mermaid logo showcases how a more complex design can work when it's tied to the brand's identity. It represents the seafaring history of coffee and Starbucks' Seattle roots.

- **Twitter:** The Twitter logo, known as the 'Twitter Bird', is a perfect example of a logo that communicates the brand's purpose. The small, blue bird in flight symbolizes the light, quick, and everywhere nature of the platform's short messages or 'tweets'. The logo is simple, clean, and easily recognizable, embodying the straightforward and fast-paced nature of the social media platform.

- **Amazon:** The Amazon logo features a curved arrow from the letter 'A' to 'Z', representing that the company carries everything from A to Z. Additionally, the arrow has a secondary, subtle design as a smile, demonstrating Amazon's mission to make customers happy.

- **Mercedes-Benz:** The Mercedes-Benz logo, a simple three-pointed star enclosed in a circle, represents the brand's mission to provide motorized vehicles "on land, on water, and in the air." The simplicity of the logo enables it to be recognized immediately, reflecting the brand's commitment to innovation and quality.

- **Coca-Cola:** The Coca-Cola logo is a superb example of the power of distinctive typography. The flowing script has barely changed since its creation in the late 19th century, demonstrating the timeless appeal of the brand. Despite having no symbol or icon, the unique lettering makes this logo one of the most recognized worldwide.

- **Lululemon:** The Lululemon logo, an abstract interpretation of an 'A', may seem somewhat mysterious at first glance. However, its simplicity and distinctiveness make it easily recognizable. The stylized 'A' is often likened to a flipped Greek letter Omega (Ω) or a woman's hair and face. The logo's design is intentionally abstract to ignite curiosity and differentiate the brand from its competitors. The logo reflects Lululemon's mission of promoting an active lifestyle that goes beyond just clothing.

- **IBM:** The IBM logo, designed by Paul Rand, features a simple typeface with horizontal stripes running through the letters. This design element not only makes the logo unique but also represents speed and dynamism. The blue color signifies trust and dependability, key values in IBM's business as a technology and consulting corporation.

- **Toyota:** The Toyota logo is a clever piece of design. It consists of three overlapping ellipses, which symbolize the unification of the hearts of Toyota's customers with the heart of Toyota's products. Interestingly, all the letters of the company's name can be found within the logo. The logo represents the brand's commitment to quality, innovation, and customer satisfaction.

- **Lego:** The Lego logo uses bright, primary colors that attract children, its primary customer base. The word "Lego" is enclosed in a red square with a thick, yellow border. The rounded typography appears playful and friendly, representing the fun and creativity the brand encourages with its construction toys. The word "LEGO" is also an abbreviation of two Danish words, "leg godt", meaning "play well".

The design and evolution of these logos show how companies use them not only as a visual identifier but also as a communication tool to convey their brand values, mission, and identity. Drawing lessons from these iconic logos, consider the following essential factors when designing or redesigning your logo:

1. Monochrome Before Color
2. Understand Your Brand Identity
3. Typography Matters
4. Involve Your Team
5. Scalability is Key
6. Open Communication
7. Seek Feedback
8. Take Your Time

The Significance of Color Psychology

"Colors, like features, follow the changes of the emotions."

- Pablo Picasso

The strategic use of color is also evident in many successful logos. Consider the bright red and white of Coca-Cola, the soothing blue of Facebook, or the playful multicolor logo of Google. Each color evokes different emotions and perceptions, significantly influencing a brand's image. Hence, be judicious with the color palette you choose for your Dental brand.

Remember, the color palette you choose will not only influence your logo but extend to your website, office interiors, and other brand elements. Color plays an integral role in how your brand is perceived and remembered, making it a fundamental component of your brand strategy. Here's a few general ideas on the meaning of popular colors:

- **Red:** As seen in logos like Coca-Cola, red is a vibrant and exciting color. It can symbolize passion, energy, and urgency. For some, it also stimulates the appetite. In a Dental context, it might be used to make a bold impression and convey the energy and dynamism of your Dental Practice. However, it's worth noting that because red can also be associated with stop signs and warnings, it needs to be used carefully to avoid unwanted associations.

- **Blue:** Used in many technology and social media companies' logos like Facebook, blue conveys trust, reliability, and calmness. It's a favorite in healthcare, including Dentistry, due to its clean and soothing connotations. A logo in shades of blue might suggest that a Dental Practice is trustworthy and reliable.

- **Green:** Green often represents growth, freshness, and health. Its ties to nature can evoke feelings of tranquility and healing. A green logo might work well for a Dental Practice with a focus on holistic or natural Dentistry.

- **Yellow:** This color is often associated with happiness, positivity, and warmth, as can be seen in McDonald's golden arches. In a Dental logo, yellow could convey a friendly and welcoming atmosphere.

- **Black:** Black exudes sophistication, seriousness, and luxury. It could be a good choice for a high-end, boutique Dental Practice. However, it must be used carefully as it can also convey heaviness or solemnity.

- **White:** Signifying purity, simplicity, and cleanliness, white is often used in healthcare due to these associations. For Dentistry, it could symbolize the promise of a bright, white smile or a clean and sterile environment.

- **Purple:** This color is often associated with luxury, royalty, and wisdom. Purple could work well for a Dental Practice that specializes in cosmetic procedures or positions itself as a premium service.

- **Orange:** A mix of red's energy and yellow's happiness, orange often signifies creativity, warmth, and enthusiasm. It can be an attention-grabbing color for a logo.

Color does not add a pleasant quality to design - it reinforces it. Color has the power to demand your attention, influence your emotions, and evoke strong responses. In the world of Dental Marketing, the thoughtful application of color can be the silent factor that makes a prospective patient feel comforted, trust your expertise, and ultimately choose your practice over another. Understanding this silent language of colors is key to communicating the right message and creating the desired image of your Dental Brand.

For some of the Dental websites we design and develop, going with a darker color palette allows a more "Ritz Carlton" vibe aesthetic to come through. This is ideal for practices looking to attract higher-end types of Cosmetic Dentistry and Smile Makeover procedures. For other offices, perhaps going with a white and lighter shade of blue would be more appropriate.

Regardless of the services and demographics you are focusing on, make sure to work with a seasoned graphic designer to help assist in the color choices and overall brand identity for your Dental Practice.

"Colors are the smiles of nature."

- Leigh Hunt

CHAPTER 30: ELEVATING YOUR DENTAL PRACTICE THROUGH STRATEGIC DESIGN

"Everything is designed. Few things are designed well."

- Brian Reed

Design is an omnipresent force that shapes our perception of the world around us. In Dental Marketing, design takes center stage, wielding a profound impact on how your Dental Practice is perceived and the kind of patients it attracts. This chapter sheds light on the role of design in Dental Marketing, offers valuable tips for creating effective marketing materials, and shares best practices for developing a compelling website for your practice.

The Power of Design in Dental Marketing

Design is far from being just an aesthetic concern; it's a powerful communication tool that speaks volumes about your Dental Practice. It creates the first impression, lays the foundation for patient relationships, and distinguishes you in a competitive market. The saying "don't judge a book by its cover" might hold wisdom, but in the realm of business, aesthetics play an indispensable role in attracting and retaining patients.

- **First Impressions:** A professional and appealing design across all your touchpoints - website, marketing collateral, social media - communicates trustworthiness, professionalism, and competence, significantly impacting a potential patient's decision-making process.

- **Brand Differentiation:** In a market teeming with options, effective design differentiates your practice, providing a unique identity that sets you apart from competitors.

- **Enhanced Recall:** A consistent and memorable design makes your brand easily recognizable and increases brand recall, thus promoting patient loyalty and referrals.

Principles for Crafting Effective Marketing Materials

Creating standout marketing materials requires a blend of simplicity, consistency, and a clear focus on your unique selling proposition.

1. **Consistency:** Employ a uniform color scheme and typography across all your marketing materials. This consistency enhances your brand's recognizability and projects a sense of cohesion and professionalism.

2. **Quality Imagery:** Utilize high-resolution images, including photographs of your practice, team, and before-and-after images of patients, to showcase your expertise and the quality of your services.

3. **Call to Action:** Include clear and compelling calls to action, such as booking information or contact details, inviting potential patients to engage with your practice.

4. **Simplicity:** A clean, uncluttered design communicates effectively. Simplicity in design allows key messages and calls to action to stand out, improving conversion rates.

Best Practices for a Patient-Centric Website Design

Your website serves as a digital front door to your practice. It's where first impressions are formed, decisions are influenced, and relationships begin.

1. **Ease of Navigation:** Ensure your website is intuitively structured, allowing visitors to find the information they need quickly and effortlessly.

2. **Mobile-Friendly:** With the majority of internet traffic now coming from mobile devices, a mobile-responsive website is not an option but a necessity.

3. **Clear Communication:** Use clear, patient-friendly language to communicate your services, team qualifications, and practice philosophy.

The Pervasive Impact of Design

All successful businesses share a common characteristic: they understand the profound impact of good design. From Dyson's minimalistic product design to Airbnb's intuitive user interface, design forms an integral part of their success stories.

When it comes to your Dental Practice, it is no different. The design extends beyond your digital presence and into the physical space of your practice. It should provide a cohesive, pleasing, and memorable patient experience that perfectly reflects the quality and personality of your practice.

Draw inspiration from various sources, including Pinterest and Instagram, which feature beautifully designed Dental Practices from around the world. Create a space that is not just functional, but one that resonates with your patients and aligns with your brand's vibe and philosophy.

To illustrate, years ago, we were invited for an in-office consultation with a Dental Team. Their practice was warm, inviting, and brimming with a Zen-like ambiance – a stark contrast to their website, which had an outdated design and lacked unique content. The disconnect between their digital and physical presence was glaring.

Remember, the emotional vibe your brand radiates should mirror and amplify the unique qualities of your Dental Practice. This consistency ensures success in all your marketing efforts, leading to a thriving and well-loved Dental Practice.

In the realm of Dentistry, where comfort and trust are paramount, the design of your website serves not merely as a digital business card but as a welcoming smile to potential patients. It's the harmonious blend of aesthetic appeal, ease of navigation, and clear communication that transforms your site from being merely functional to an inviting portal, reflecting the care and professionalism patients can expect when they walk through your office doors.

CHAPTER 31: MASTERING THE ART OF BRANDING YOUR DENTAL PRACTICE

"Your brand is the single most important investment you can make in your business."

- Steve Forbes

Choosing a fitting name and slogan for your Dental Office is akin to naming a newborn - it calls for careful thought, creativity, and an understanding of the identity you wish to establish. Beyond the name, your brand encapsulates your practice's core values, personality, and promises. This chapter will guide you through the essential steps of creating a compelling Dental Practice brand, effectively managing your intellectual property, and ensuring your brand's pervasive presence in the world.

The Genesis: Choosing the Right Name and Slogan

Your Dental Office's name and slogan provide the initial glimpse into your brand. The perfect name is descriptive yet succinct, while the slogan encapsulates your brand promise in a catchy, memorable phrase. Keep in mind that the name should ideally have a corresponding available ".com" web domain for a unified online presence.

1. **Descriptive and Short:** A name that hints at your services or values, while being concise and easy to remember, works best.
2. **Availability of Domain:** Check the availability of a corresponding ".com" domain for your website. If it's unavailable, consider purchasing it from aftermarket or at a premium price.

3. **Timeless:** Envision your practice in the future. Will the name still hold relevance if someone else takes over?

4. **Secure Usernames and IP addresses:** Once the name is decided, register related usernames and IP addresses across all platforms, including Instagram, Facebook, Twitter, etc.

To navigate this process smoothly, you might consider hiring a branding agency. These professionals can help brainstorm potential names, craft a slogan, and secure all the assets needed to establish your brand.

Living Your Brand: From Digital Presence to Real-World Interaction

It's not enough for your brand to exist only on your website or social media. Your brand should be a living, breathing entity, visible in your office, Team, and marketing efforts. Here's how you can make it happen:

1. **Brand Your Dental Team:** Uniforms with your logo create a sense of unity and professionalism. Ensure the uniforms are comfortable and stylish, representing your brand ethos. To add a personal touch, you might consider letting team members choose a number to embroider on their uniforms, much like athletes do.

2. **Business Cards for Team Members:** Empower your team to be brand ambassadors by providing personalized business cards. This simple tool can help spread the word about your practice at various events and interactions.

3. **Brand Presence at Local Events:** Take part in local events and sponsorships, ensuring your brand is visible and active in your community. This enhances brand recognition and reinforces your commitment to the community you serve.

Safeguarding Your Brand: Managing Your Intellectual Property

While creating and promoting your brand is crucial, protecting it is equally, if not more, essential. In this digital era, intellectual property (IP) management plays a significant role in brand preservation.

1. **Domain Ownership:** Always maintain full access and ownership of your domain name. While you can delegate access to your web developer or marketing agency, retain complete control.

2. **Access to Social Media Accounts:** Similarly, keep login details and admin access to all your social media accounts. Grant roles like manager or editor to others, but maintain ownership to avoid potential problems.

Understanding and controlling your IP is a crucial step in your practice's digital security. While not the most exciting aspect of marketing, it's fundamentally essential. If you don't have access to your website or social media, your marketing efforts are hamstrung.

Your brand is the most potent tool you possess to carve a niche in the Dental industry. A well-crafted and well-maintained brand resonates with your target audience, earning their trust and loyalty in the local community. Hence, invest your time, effort, and resources wisely to create, promote, and preserve your brand. Remember, your brand should always reflect the authenticity and uniqueness of your practice, letting it thrive in the competitive marketplace.

CHAPTER 32: IS YOUR DENTAL PRACTICE INSTAGRAMMABLE?

"In the world of Instagram, the only limit to success is your own creativity."

– Anonymous

In the dynamic world of social media, one platform has indisputably transformed the way businesses market themselves: Instagram. Its unique selling point lies in its visual-centric content, where businesses from all sectors, including Dentistry, capitalize on aesthetics to attract engagement and foster a brand community. A strategy that has gained traction in this realm is 'Instagrammification.' But what does it mean, and how can it be a game-changer for your Dental Practice?

Instagrammification represents the creation of aesthetically appealing and eye-catching spaces within your establishment that spark customers' interest to capture and share photos on Instagram. Typically, this strategy has been employed by industries such as hospitality and retail, but its essence holds vast potential for Dentistry as well.

Imagine transforming a portion of your Dental Practice into an Instagrammable corner. The reception area, for instance, is a prime candidate for such an endeavor. It could feature an engaging quote, relevant to Dentistry, such as, "They sure are handy when you smile, so keep your teeth around a while," - Dr. Seuss. This quote could be made prominent by using a vibrant neon sign.

But the transformation doesn't stop with a sign. The setting could be enriched with a draping of natural ivy over the sign. The lush green will not only add to the overall aesthetics but also lend a calming, soothing element to the environment. Consider lighting up the sign area strategically to accentuate the quote, drawing attention and making it perfect for a snapshot.

Comfort is another crucial aspect to consider. Adorn this space with comfortable seating, such as a plush couch or trendy chairs. The idea is to create an atmosphere that's not only visually appealing but also inviting, making patients feel at ease and inclined to engage.

Designing this Instagrammable spot needs to be done with mobile phone users in mind. Given the way people rapidly scroll through their feeds, it's important to ensure that the spot stands out and is easily readable on small screens. Everything from the size of the neon sign to the color contrast should be thoughtfully selected to make a lasting impact even in a quick glance.

If your Dental Practice caters to children, infusing elements of fun and whimsy into your Instagrammable spot can be a great idea. A wall adorned with vibrant illustrations of friendly toothbrushes, toothpaste, and other Dental-related cartoons can be a hit. This not only encourages photo opportunities but also helps in easing children's apprehensions about Dental visits.

While the concept might sound daunting, bringing in a local interior designer can be an effective solution. Their expertise can help achieve your vision of an Instagrammable corner that embodies your brand, aligns with your aesthetics, and doesn't require a full-scale renovation.

In essence, Instagrammification is about creating a physical space that captures attention, triggers patient engagement, and promotes your brand. By doing so, your Dental Practice can heighten its social media presence and engagement, enticing current and prospective patients. Remember, a small investment in interior design and branding can yield significant results in your overall Dental marketing efforts. Now the question remains - is your Dental Practice Instagrammable? If not, it's time to make it one.

CHAPTER 33: HARNESSING THE POWER OF THREADS IN DENTAL MARKETING

"Each thread in the digital tapestry we weave, like Threads, has the power to connect, engage, and inspire. It's our responsibility to use this power wisely, to shape the narratives that our threads tell."

- *Anonymous*

Dental Marketing isn't just an exercise in advertising, it's a canvas where we paint stories. These narratives echo with the transformative power of Dental care - stories that speak of the joy of a restored smile, the regained self-esteem that follows improved Dental health, the relief that emerges from the resolution of chronic Dental discomfort. Our endeavor in Dental Marketing is not just to churn out these stories, but to ensure they are heard, comprehended, and cherished.

In this journey, Meta's latest digital platform, Threads, has emerged as an enabler. Threads empowers us to craft, share, and amplify our narratives more effectively, opening up a new world of possibilities for Dental Marketing.

At first glance, Threads might appear similar to Twitter, yet the vision Meta holds for it is vastly different. Threads isn't just another social media platform; it's a place conceived to inspire positive, engaging, and meaningful conversations. It's like Twitter, but with a heart that pulsates with hope, making it a fitting stage for uplifting stories to unfold and resonate.

Deciphering Threads

Threads is a trailblazing app designed to fuel public discourse through the sharing of text updates. With a single set of Instagram credentials, you can weave stories through a combination of text, images, and video posts. Each post offers a canvas of up to 500 characters and allows for videos of up to 5 minutes. But that's not all; Threads even lets you share relevant links to enrich your narrative. And to truly democratize digital dialogue, Instagram aspires to seamlessly integrate Threads with other open, interoperable social networks. This marks a pivotal shift in the digital communication paradigm, ushering in an era of unified, interactive dialogues.

Empowering Dental Marketing with Threads

1. **Crafting Engaging Content**

   To truly touch the hearts of your audience, you need to speak their language. Unearth and curate content that resonates with your patients - whether it's updates about your Dental Practice, an insider view into Dental procedures, easy-to-follow Dental hygiene tips, or heartwarming patient success stories. Ensure that every piece of content you put out is a faithful reflection of your brand ethos, creating a consistent and compelling narrative across all platforms.

2. **Understanding Your Audience**

   Even as Threads amplifies your voice, reaching out to a broader audience, it's crucial to retain an in-depth understanding of your target demographic. Tailored content is a cornerstone of meaningful engagement. As you navigate this unexplored territory of social media, make it a point to align your content strategy with the goals you wish to achieve.

3. **Driving Engagement**

   Engagement isn't just about disseminating content; it's about fostering two-way interactions. Challenge your audience to engage with your posts; stimulate dialogue by posing questions, inviting opinions, and ensuring that you are quick to acknowledge their responses. Higher reach and engagement often trigger organic growth, an observation that rings true across Meta's platforms like Facebook and Instagram.

4. Evaluating and Adapting

As you set out on this journey, don't forget to pack your compass: engagement metrics on Threads. These metrics help you decipher what content truly clicks with your audience. Armed with these insights, you can refine your strategy for improved results. By viewing these metrics holistically, you can chart out a well-defined path to leveraging this platform effectively.

Threads, with its unique focus on text-based updates, public conversations, and interoperability, is set to redefine the social media landscape. By integrating Threads into your Dental Marketing strategy, you open up new avenues to cultivate an engaged, diverse patient community. Embrace Threads, and let your Dental Practice shine brightly as a beacon in this ever-evolving digital landscape. Your story deserves to be told; let Threads be your narrator.

CHAPTER 34: A DEEPER DIVE INTO DENTAL MEMBERSHIPS - UNLEASHING POTENTIAL AND EXPANDING PATIENT CARE

"Quality healthcare should be a basic right, not a luxury limited to the wealthy."

- Mary Otto, Oral Health Journalist.

Introduction to Dental Memberships

Dental Memberships are revolutionizing the healthcare industry, making comprehensive Dental care accessible and affordable. By signing up for these memberships, patients unlock the gateway to preventative care and significant discounts on various procedures, ranging from routine check-ups, cleanings, and X-rays, to fillings, crowns, and orthodontic work. Furthermore, certain Dental Memberships extend unique privileges, such as emergency care and after-hours access to the dentist.

The Dual Advantage of Dental Memberships

These memberships are a win-win for both Dentists and patients. While patients enjoy a suite of benefits and access to affordable care, Dentists can foster patient loyalty, ensure a steady flow of income, and potentially broaden their patient base. The challenge, however, lies in marketing these membership plans effectively to the right patients.

Segment One: Understanding Your Patient Demographics

Before embarking on the marketing journey, it's essential to understand your patient demographics, including age, income, and Dental needs. This knowledge enables you to custom-tailor your marketing strategy, reaching the patients most likely to be interested in a Dental Membership.

For instance, if a significant portion of your patients are seniors on a fixed income, you might want to emphasize the cost-saving aspect of the membership. Conversely, if your practice serves many young families, accentuating the comprehensive care and preventative benefits could be more appealing.

Segment Two: Communicating the Benefits of Dental Memberships

After understanding your target audience, the next phase is to communicate the benefits of Dental Memberships effectively. Use various marketing channels like brochures, website content, social media, and in-office promotions to spread the message. Focus on the direct benefits that patients will receive, such as cost savings, comprehensive care, and the convenience of regular check-ups and cleanings.

Segment Three: Incentives and Special Promotions: The Art of Attraction

One effective strategy to promote Dental Memberships involves offering incentives and special promotions. Offering discounted rates for new members or a free consultation to prospective members can spur interest. Additionally, creating a referral strategy for patients who recommend your practice to their friends and family can help attract new patients while rewarding your existing ones.

Segment Four: Streamlining the Sign-Up Process

Simplify the sign-up process to ensure a smooth transition for your patients. Provide clear, easy-to-understand information about membership plans and flexible payment options. Having a dedicated Team member to answer any queries can help make the process seamless and ensure patients feel comfortable and confident in their decision to sign up for a Dental Membership.

One platform to consider for managing your Dental membership plan is Kleer. Kleer offers an intuitive and user-friendly platform for both patients and Dentists, making Dental Membership management a breeze. We work with our clients to properly implement Kleer and it's been a huge boost to the overall success of their membership plan growth.

Dental Memberships can be a powerful tool for offices to provide patients with more affordable and comprehensive care. By understanding your patient demographics, communicating the benefits of Dental Memberships, offering incentives and special promotions, and streamlining the sign-up process, you can successfully market Dental Memberships and enhance your practice.

"It is not your customer's job to remember you, it is your obligation and responsibility to make sure they don't have the chance to forget you."

- Patricia Fripp

CHAPTER 35: AMPLIFYING YOUR DENTAL PRACTICE THROUGH REFERRAL MARKETING

"Happy customers are your biggest advocates and can become your most successful sales team."

- Lisa Masiello

Introduction to Referral Marketing for Dental Practices

The efficacy of Referral Marketing has not gone unnoticed in the world of Dental Practices. This potent tool transforms the traditional patient-doctor relationship into a powerful partnership. It encourages existing patients to become ambassadors of your Dental Practice, recommending your services to their friends and family. This chapter aims to shed light on the vast benefits of Referral Marketing, offer effective strategies to create a referral program, and share actionable tips to elevate the efficiency of a referral marketing campaign.

Why Dental Practices Should Embrace Referral Marketing

"A satisfied customer is the best business strategy of all."

- Michael LeBoeuf

Referral Marketing hinges on the most vital of human instincts: trust. When a potential patient hears of your Dental Practice from someone they trust, they are considerably more inclined to book an appointment. Referral Marketing, therefore, tends to be highly cost-effective, providing exceptional returns without substantial investment in conventional advertising campaigns.

Crafting a Robust Referral Program: A Strategy Primer

Building a Referral Program that yields significant results requires strategic planning. Offering referral incentives to existing patients, such as discounts on subsequent visits or small tokens of appreciation, can be effective.

To further enhance the ease and effectiveness of the process, consider distributing referral cards or incorporating a user-friendly referral form on your practice's website. The power of social media can also be harnessed to promote your referral program, motivating patients to share their referral links with their wider network.

Turbocharging Your Referral Marketing Campaign

Elevating the performance of your Referral Marketing campaign demands a commitment to nurturing strong relationships with your patients. Provide exceptional customer service, engage with patients through consistent email communications and social media interactions, and request feedback about their experiences.

Promote your referral program proactively. Include detailed information about it in patient welcome kits and follow-up communications. Consistent promotion can result in an increase in referrals and, ultimately, new patients for your practice.

The Power of Word-of-Mouth

In the landscape of Dental Practices, Referral Marketing is an invaluable tool. By enabling satisfied patients to bring in new clientele from their circles, we tap into the immense power of word-of-mouth marketing.

With a well-conceived referral program, persistent promotion, and strong patient relationships, your practice can maximize its referral marketing campaign's impact, expanding both patient base and reputation.

The easiest way to encourage more word-of-mouth referrals from existing patients is to place signage in your reception area. Design a beautiful sign that reminds patients you are accepting new patients, along with expressing your appreciation for sharing the love of your office to their own friends and family.

"The purpose of a business is to create a customer who creates customers."
- Shiv Singh

One of the pivotal strategies for increasing patient referrals in your Dental Practice involves crafting unforgettable patient experiences, combined with creating compelling "talking points". Consider the example of the DoubleTree hotel chain and their signature approach to guest hospitality. On every check-in, guests receive complimentary chocolate chip cookies. This simple yet delightful gesture has become a defining characteristic of their brand, influencing many people's decision to choose DoubleTree hotels. The anticipation of a warm, delicious treat upon arrival adds a unique element to their stay, creating a lasting memory that they're eager to share with others. Although specific statistics aren't available, this initiative is well-known and has certainly contributed to their brand loyalty and customer satisfaction.

Drawing from this, it's critical for your Dental Practice to identify and establish your own equivalent of the "chocolate chip cookie" moment. This could be anything from offering soothing music during treatments, introducing a play area for patients' children, presenting personalized post-treatment care packages, or even just showcasing exceptional interpersonal communication.

When you provide an experience that exceeds expectations, your Dental Patients will remember their visits positively and will be more inclined to mention your practice in conversations with friends, family, and colleagues. The key is to make these "talking points" as distinctive and personalized as possible to differentiate your Dental Practice from others.

By curating these memorable experiences, your Dental Practice can generate a consistent influx of patient referrals, thereby cementing your reputation and promoting long-term growth. Remember, people love to share their incredible experiences, and word-of-mouth marketing is one of the most powerful and cost-effective ways to attract new Dental Patients and enhance your practice's visibility in the community.

CHAPTER 36: SETTING YOUR MARKETING GOALS AND OBJECTIVES

"Setting goals is the first step in turning the invisible into the visible."

- Tony Robbins

In any marketing strategy, the first step is to define your goals and objectives. These will serve as your guiding star throughout your journey, helping to focus your efforts and measure your success. This chapter will walk you through how to set effective and actionable goals for your Dental Marketing strategy.

The Importance of Goals and Objectives

Before we dive into how to set your goals, let's understand their significance in marketing. Goals and objectives provide clarity and direction, helping you to prioritize your actions, allocate resources, and make decisions effectively. They act as the foundation of your Dental Marketing plan, influencing every other aspect of your strategy.

SMART Goals

A helpful approach to goal-setting is to use the SMART framework, which stands for Specific, Measurable, Achievable, Relevant, and Time-bound. Let's break down what each of these means:

- **Specific:** Your goals should be clear and detailed. Instead of saying "I want to attract more patients," a specific goal might be "I want to attract 30 new patients each month."

- **Measurable:** How will you know when you've reached your goal? It's crucial to have a way to track your progress.

- **Achievable:** Your goals should be challenging but still within reach. Setting unrealistic goals can lead to disappointment and demotivation.

- **Relevant:** Your goals should align with your practice's overall vision and objectives.

- **Time-bound:** Setting a timeframe for your goals creates a sense of urgency and can motivate you to stay on track.

Defining Your Marketing Objectives

Your marketing objectives should align with your goals and serve as the steps to achieve them. For instance, if your goal is to attract 30 new patients each month, objectives might include increasing website traffic by 30%, boosting social media engagement by 25%, or increasing conversion rates by 15%.

Setting Key Performance Indicators (KPIs)

KPIs help you measure the success of your marketing objectives. They are the metrics that you will track to determine if your efforts are moving you closer to your goals. For example, the KPIs for the above objectives could be the number of website visits, social media likes and shares, and the number of inquiries or appointments booked.

Setting clear and actionable goals and objectives is a critical first step in any Dental Marketing strategy. By defining what you want to achieve, how you'll measure success, and the steps you'll take to get there, you set the foundation for a successful marketing plan. Remember the words of famed management consultant Peter Drucker: "What gets measured gets managed." By setting, tracking, and managing your goals and objectives, you put yourself on the path to success.

Additionally, making sure all of your Dental Team members are involved in this entire process will be enormously beneficial to the realization of your goals and objectives.

CHAPTER 37: NAVIGATING THE RETURN ON INVESTMENT IN YOUR DENTAL MARKETING PLAN

Venturing into the intricate world of marketing, there is an axiom that resonates widely: "You cannot refine what you cannot measure." When you dissect this, it becomes crystal clear how relevant this is to your Return on Investment (ROI). In this chapter, we will illuminate the path to proficiently monitor and comprehend the ROI of your Dental Marketing Plan, an essential ingredient in the recipe for your practice's prosperity.

Decoding ROI

The acronym 'ROI' refers to "Return on Investment," a vital gauge of your marketing undertakings' efficacy. In a nutshell, it illustrates what you're gaining in return for the resources you've invested into your marketing blueprint. A positive ROI signals that your marketing maneuvers are fruitful, while a negative ROI could be a warning sign to reassess or alter your approach.

The Imperative Role of ROI Tracking

Gauging the ROI of your Dental Marketing scheme aids in pinpointing the triumphant strategies and those needing a tweak, thus enabling you to fine-tune your marketing expenditure and operations. It imparts valuable knowledge which can steer your practice's decision-making and strategy formulation.

Calculating ROI

The fundamental equation for ROI is: (Net Profit / Total Investment) * 100. In Dental marketing terms, net profit might equate to the income generated from new patients procured through marketing endeavors, while total investment would represent your comprehensive marketing expenditure.

Nevertheless, deciphering the ROI of your marketing plan extends beyond merely manipulating numbers in a formula. It entails tracking vital metrics, comprehending your patient journey, and leveraging the correct tools and software.

Crucial Metrics for Monitoring

The crucial metrics to monitor hinge on your specific aims and strategies, but could encompass:

- **Cost of Patient Acquisition:** What is the average cost to procure a new patient through your marketing endeavors?

- **Patient's Lifetime Value:** How much income does a patient contribute to your practice throughout their tenure with you?

- **Conversion Rate:** What fraction of prospective patients (leads) eventually become actual patients?

- **Patient Retention Rate:** What fraction of patients consistently return to your practice?

Harnessing Analytics Tools

Contemporary analytics tools like Google Analytics or specialized Dental Practice management software can offer a treasure trove of data and simplify tracking ROI. They allow you to measure site traffic, monitor conversion rates, and scrutinize patient behavior, among other functions.

Comprehending the ROI of your Dental Marketing plan goes beyond mere number crunching. It's about delving into your marketing performance insights that facilitate informed decisions and strategic realignments. According to HubSpot's study, organizations that calculate ROI have a 72% likelihood of having an effective marketing strategy. Meanwhile, only 49% of businesses that do not measure ROI claim their strategies are effective, revealing a clear-cut edge in ROI tracking.

Moreover, research from the Content Marketing Institute reveals that consistent ROI measurers are the most triumphant marketers. Approximately 80% of the high-achieving businesses are intent on realizing marketing ROI, a contrast to the mere 57% of the least triumphant.

As we remember the words of noted business philosopher Jim Rohn, "Either you run the day or the day runs you." By understanding and measuring ROI meticulously, you seize the reins of your Dental Marketing strategy, propelling it towards growth and triumph.

When strategizing with your marketing person or agency, constantly obsess about analytics, data and ROI across all channels. This will allow you to better understand what's working and what's not, so everyone can make more well informed decisions.

CHAPTER 38: AUGMENTED REALITY - REVOLUTIONIZING DENTAL MARKETING

"Any sufficiently advanced technology is indistinguishable from magic," Arthur C. Clarke once said. In the realm of Dental Marketing, the 'magic' is found in Augmented Reality (AR), a technology that seamlessly blends digital elements into our real world. By taking a leap of faith into AR, Dental Practices can redefine patient experiences and supercharge their marketing efforts.

Augmented Reality Demystified

Augmented Reality works by overlaying digital information - images, sounds, or other data - onto the real world, enhancing the user's perception and interaction with their environment. With AR, potential patients can visualize Dental procedures, understand complex concepts, or even preview their smile transformation - all in a highly engaging and interactive manner.

AR in Smile Simulation

One of the most exciting applications of AR in Dental Marketing is smile simulation. It allows potential patients to 'try on' their new smile virtually, before committing to a procedure. This experience can significantly reduce anxiety and build patient confidence, increasing the likelihood of them choosing your practice for their treatment.

AR for Patient Education

Augmented Reality can also play a pivotal role in patient education, making complex Dental procedures easy to understand. For instance, an AR application could help a patient visualize how a Dental implant is placed, how braces correct alignment, or how proper brushing techniques can prevent cavities. By demystifying Dental procedures, AR enhances patient trust and communication, which can translate into better patient relationships and improved treatment acceptance.

AR in Office Tours

A virtual office tour using AR can give potential patients a feel for your practice before they even step foot inside. This interactive experience, showcasing your office layout, equipment, and ambiance, can help to break down barriers and ease anxieties, making patients feel more comfortable even before their first visit.

Implementing AR

Integrating AR into your marketing strategy requires planning and investment. You'll need to collaborate with AR developers to create engaging, user-friendly experiences. Also, remember to train your team on how to leverage these tools effectively, and inform your patients about these tech advancements via your marketing channels.

AR technology holds the promise of transforming the way Dental Practices market themselves and interact with their patients. The integration of AR into Dental Marketing strategies provides a unique, engaging, and highly personalized patient experience. It's an investment that has the potential to set a practice apart from the competition and steer it towards unprecedented growth. As tech entrepreneur Elon Musk rightly said, "The first step is to establish that something is possible; then probability will occur." Are you ready to embrace the possibilities with Augmented Reality in your Dental Marketing strategy?

Leading technology companies are releasing exciting products that will completely revolutionize how we all interact with each other both online and offline. This provides a very exciting opportunity to market your Dental Practice uniquely, courageously and authentically.

CHAPTER 39: DESTINATION DENTAL VISITORS - ATTRACTING OUT-OF-TOWN PATIENTS

In the era of Cosmetic Dentistry and smile makeovers, a new trend has emerged: Destination Dental Visits. This model is akin to medical tourism, where individuals travel to receive Dental care and enjoy a vacation concurrently. This has proven to be particularly lucrative for higher-end Cosmetic Dentistry services, where the expertise of the Dentist and the allure of a picturesque location merge into an attractive package.

Targeting the Right Audience

To attract out-of-town visitors, your Dental Practice needs to target the right audience. These are typically individuals who value quality over cost and seek superior Dental care experiences. Focus your marketing efforts on highlighting your Team's expertise, state-of-the-art facilities, advanced technologies, and the wide range of cosmetic services you offer.

According to Patients Beyond Borders, a leading information resource for Medical tourism, an estimated 1.9 million Americans will travel annually outside the U.S. for medical care. Imagine tapping into a fraction of this market by offering a local, more convenient alternative with the same allure of combining Dental treatment and vacation.

Creating a Unique Value Proposition

Dental Practices looking to attract this audience need to offer a unique value proposition. This involves crafting a seamless, all-encompassing package that covers all aspects of the patient's journey — from the initial consultation to post-treatment care. Offer assistance in travel arrangements, accommodation booking, and local sightseeing. The aim is to provide an unforgettable experience that goes beyond excellent Dental care.

Leveraging Digital Marketing

Harness the power of digital marketing to reach out to potential out-of-town patients. Share patient testimonials, before-and-after photos, and informative content about your Cosmetic Dentistry and smile makeover services on your website and social media channels. Invest in SEO and geo-targeted PPC campaigns to increase your visibility among potential patients planning destination Dental visits.

Building Partnerships

Collaborate with local businesses such as hotels, travel agencies, and tourist attractions to create attractive travel packages. This not only enhances your patients' experience but also drives local economic growth.

While destination Dental visits might be a relatively new trend, it's a rapidly growing one that represents a unique business opportunity. In the words of Guy Kawasaki, "Opportunities are like sunrises. If you wait too long, you miss them." So don't wait — position your practice now as the go-to destination for high-end Cosmetic Dentistry and smile makeover services.

As more people become aware of the possibilities of combining Dental care with travel, the demand for such services will only grow. By harnessing this trend, you can elevate your practice to new heights and significantly enhance your patients' experience — all while enjoying the rewards of catering to a high-end market segment.

CHAPTER 40: IMPLEMENTING IN-OFFICE SEMINARS TO STAND-OUT AND ATTRACT NEW PATIENTS

In the competitive world of Dentistry, continually innovating to attract and retain patients is critical. One potent strategy to consider is implementing in-office seminars. These educational sessions provide the platform to exhibit your expertise and offer potential and current patients insights into various Dental services, procedures, and technologies. This chapter explores the strategy and execution behind these seminars to effectively distinguish your practice and attract new patients.

Why In-Office Seminars?

In-office seminars are a distinctive opportunity to educate the public about oral-health and showcase your expertise. By bringing potential patients into your Dental Office, these events allow them to familiarize themselves with your Team, services, and environment.

In-office seminars confer multiple benefits. They position your Dental Office as a beacon in oral-health education, build community relationships, differentiate your practice from competitors, and most importantly, draw in new patients.

Planning Your Seminars

Choosing the day and time for your seminar is crucial to maximizing attendance. From our experience helping to promote these in-office seminars for clients, research indicates that conducting seminars on Thursdays for lunch or evening, or Saturdays from 10 AM - 11 AM, are optimal to accommodate the schedules of working professionals and families. Always make sure to provide some light refreshments and snacks, ideally from a local restaurant. This allows you to also capture social media content during the events and mention these restaurants.

Themes and Topics

The choice of seminar topic is of paramount importance. Showcasing services like Dental Sleep Apnea, Cosmetic Dentistry, and Smile Makeovers can cater to a wider interest group and demonstrate the breadth of your practice's services.

- **Dental Sleep Apnea:** A seminar focusing on this prevalent, yet under-recognized condition, can educate attendees about its diagnosis, treatment, and the importance of timely intervention, establishing your practice as a leader in this area.

- **Cosmetic Dentistry and Smile Makeovers:** The universal desire for an attractive smile ensures these topics will appeal to a broad audience. Ranging from those contemplating minor aesthetic enhancements to individuals interested in complete smile transformations, these seminars can reveal the transformative power of Cosmetic Dentistry. Utilizing before-and-after cases from your practice can illustrate potential results effectively.

Marketing Your Seminars

Once you've defined your seminar topics and schedule, your next step is marketing. Use a combination of online and offline strategies, including your website, social media channels, email newsletters, direct mail, and local advertising. Patient testimonials and before-and-after photos can bolster credibility and interest.

One effective tool to consider is Eventbrite, an online ticketing platform. It not only facilitates ticket distribution but also serves as another channel for promoting your event and managing RSVPs. Because your in-office seminars are free to attend, there are no costs involved with using Eventbrite.

Hosting Your Seminars

On the day of the seminar, ensure your office exudes an inviting atmosphere. Aim to make the session interactive and engaging through a mix of presentations, Q&As, and hands-on demonstrations. Having brochures and take-home materials readily available can reinforce your message and remind attendees of your services.

After the seminar, follow up with attendees via email or phone calls, thank them for their participation, seek their feedback, and encourage them to schedule an appointment.

Remember the words of author and motivational speaker, Chris Grosser: "Opportunities don't happen, you create them." In-office seminars are an incredible opportunity not just to educate the community but to meet and connect with potential patients. After all, as Grosser says, "Success usually comes to those who are too busy to be looking for it."

Implementing in-office seminars is a powerful marketing tool for Dental Practices. By positioning your practice as a leader in Dental Health education and displaying your expertise, you can stand out from the competition and attract new patients. Carefully plan, market, and execute your seminars to ensure their success and deliver value to attendees.

CHAPTER 41: YOUR NEXT STEPS - MASTERING THE ART OF DENTAL MARKETING

"Marketing is not just about the stuff that you make, but about the story you tell."

- Tarang Shah

Reflecting on the Journey

Congratulations! You've journeyed through this comprehensive guide, armed yourself with knowledge, and are now prepared to revolutionize your Dental Practice's marketing efforts. Take a moment to reflect on the vast insights you've gathered, and remember, progress rather than perfection.

In many instances, the biggest obstacles in marketing are not external but are the ones we place in our path. As you dive headlong into your Dental Marketing journey, be conscious of these barriers. Remember, even tasks that seem daunting at first, like video marketing, can become a boon for your practice with the right mindset and strategies.

Harnessing the Power of Video Marketing

Video marketing is a potent tool that opens up a treasure trove of opportunities, especially for specialties like Cosmetic Dentistry and Implant Dentistry. Tap into the video formats and content ideas provided in this guide, and remember the golden rule: Shoot more content than you need so that you can repurpose it from multiple angles. Authenticity and purposeful storytelling are key elements that will resonate with your viewers.

Mastering SEO and Conversion Rate Optimization

Maximizing your Dental Practice's online visibility is integral to attracting and converting patients. By mastering the art of Search Engine Optimization (SEO) and enhancing your Conversion Rate, you'll place your practice in the spotlight. Complementing an effective SEO strategy with Pay-Per-Click (PPC) advertising can help expand your online reach. Combined with astute Conversion Rate Optimization, these strategies will transform sporadic bookings into a consistently busy schedule.

Building Trust and Influence

As you solidify your marketing momentum, remember the power of social listening. Engaging with your viewers, followers, fans, and patients - both existing and prospective - will help you stay relevant and maintain their trust. Use our Paid Ad Tips for Success to capitalize on your social media presence and reach potential new patients who are looking for a practitioner just like you.

Embracing the Marketing Spectrum

To succeed in today's dynamic marketing landscape, embracing a blend of Digital Marketing, AI Marketing, and Traditional Marketing is crucial. Keep your content fresh and inspired, and success will follow. Plan ahead and accumulate a library of user-generated content and in-house-created content.

Even if you're a one-person marketing team, remember, you have the tools and knowledge to craft an effective marketing strategy. Remember, blending traditional and digital marketing strategies can help you meet your potential new patients wherever they are.

Empowering Your Team and Protecting Your Brand

"Brand is just a perception, and perception will match reality over time."

- Elon Musk

Finally, empower your team and protect your Dental Brand. You're not just building a business; you're creating an identity, a reputation. This identity should precede you in the office and in the wider world.

In the ever-evolving landscape of marketing, embracing innovation, creativity, and technology is more than just a strategy; it's a necessity. As we conclude this guide, our hope is that you feel equipped and inspired to navigate this dynamic world, employing tools ranging from logo design and website development to Local SEO and beyond.

The concept of 'Dentainment,' merging Dental education and entertainment, is transforming patient interactions, breaking down barriers, and fostering stronger relationships. As you look towards the future, we encourage you to embrace this trend, creating engaging, informative, and enjoyable experiences for your patients.

At the heart of our commitment to you is the promise to stay at the forefront of these shifts, continually updating our knowledge and skills to serve you better. We're not just here to guide you through your marketing journey; we're here to walk it with you, providing cutting-edge digital marketing services tailored to the unique needs of your particular Dental Practice.

THANK YOU for choosing to embark on this expedition with us. It has been our pleasure to share our expertise, and we look forward to continuing this journey together, striving towards the common goal of growing your practice and creating inspiring, lasting impressions in the minds of your patients. Your journey to greater visibility, patient engagement, and success is just beginning, and we're excited to see where it takes you.

We hope that you'll take these insights, strategies, and tips to heart, implementing them into your marketing initiatives to yield tangible, prosperous results. We encourage you to stay curious, always seeking to learn and improve. After all, the best marketers are those who never cease to learn.

Most importantly, never lose sight of the central goal in all of this: creating a truly remarkable patient experience. Every marketing decision you make should ultimately serve this purpose. As you grow your practice, continue to keep your patients at the heart of all you do. After all, they are the lifeblood of your practice.

We can't wait to hear about the extraordinary milestones and successes you will undoubtedly achieve. Keep striving, keep innovating, and most importantly, keep making those unforgettable smiles. Thanks again for letting us be part of your journey towards marketing excellence in the Dental care you provide to patients.

ABOUT THE AUTHOR AND AGENCY THAT BROUGHT YOU BEST DENTAL MARKETING:

Brad Newman, Founder & Chief Buzz Officer of Dentainment

Brad Newman, an entrepreneur since childhood, is a recognized leader in marketing and business development for Dental Practices. His unique insights and strategic approach stem from a rich tapestry of entrepreneurial adventures, including his very first venture, B&B Car Wash, launched at the tender age of 14 with a childhood friend. Even at this early stage, Brad was in charge of marketing, honing skills that would prove indispensable in his future endeavors.

Through Dentainment, Brad marries his deep understanding of marketing with his passion for promoting oral health. His enthusiasm, creativity, and dedication are palpable, making him an extraordinary force in this critical field. Helping people connect with top-notch Dental Practices and receive quality Dental Care is not just his profession—it's his mission.

Over the years, Brad's entrepreneurial journey has spanned diverse platforms, from summer hockey camps and consumer products to innovative internet properties that he has built, nurtured, and sold. In all these ventures, generating "BUZZ" and pioneering marketing strategies were pivotal to their success, a testament to Brad's marketing acumen.

Beyond his professional accomplishments, Brad is an ardent hockey enthusiast. Having started playing at just four years old, his love for the sport led him to play college hockey at Bowling Green State University and professionally in Italy. Outside the rink, Brad savors a good cup of coffee, relishes sushi, and finds peace in practicing yoga. A man of many passions, Brad continues to be an inspiring force in Dental Practice marketing.

Dentainment: A Pioneer in Customized Dental Marketing Solutions

Established in 2010, Dentainment is a boutique digital marketing agency specializing in serving Dental Practices. Our journey began in Santa Monica, CA, with our first client, Dr. Beverly, setting the stage for our mission: To help Dental Practices attract new patients, increase revenues, and build brand equity through innovative, multi-channel marketing solutions.

At Dentainment, we believe in a unique, tailored approach to marketing – "template" is not a part of our vocabulary. Our strategies are built upon a blend of cutting-edge technology, such as Artificial Intelligence (AI), and our profound understanding of the Dental industry. Our services encompass Video Content Creation, Social Media Management, Website Design, and Marketing Consulting, among others.

Our founder, Brad Newman, also known as our Chief Buzz Officer, together with our dedicated Team, has built the company on pride, passion, and professionalism. We are not just an agency; we are practitioners, creators, and partners, committed to providing the best marketing and brand-building services for Dental Practices.

Over the years, we have had the privilege of working with an array of clients, from the world's most famous Cosmetic Dentist and remarkable Dental Associations to Master Clinician Dental Implant Courses. We value all our partnerships, and we extend our heartfelt gratitude to the incredible Dental Teams and mentors we have collaborated with over the years.

Our track record includes significantly enhancing our clients' online presence and boosting their new patient numbers. In the ever-evolving digital age, Dentainment stands as a trusted ally for Dental Practices looking to navigate the complex terrain of Dental marketing. Our commitment to customized marketing solutions and our knack for creating engaging digital platforms set us apart in the world of Dental Marketing.

DENTAL MARKETING PLAN WORKSHEETS

Practice Overview

- Briefly describe your practice.

- Conduct a SWOT Analysis. (You can revisit this every few months to identify any changes.)

Target Audience

- Describe your target patients (Include age, demographics, psychographics).

- List the unique needs or concerns of your target patients.

Unique Selling Proposition (USP)

- Define what sets your practice apart from the competition.
- Explain why patients should choose your practice over others.

Marketing Goals

- Outline your SMART (Specific, Measurable, Achievable, Relevant, Time-bound) marketing goals for the upcoming year.

- Regularly revisit these goals to assess your progress.

Online Marketing Strategies

- Write down the online marketing strategies you plan to use (website, SEO, content marketing, social media, email marketing).

- For each strategy, outline the specific tactics you plan to use.

Offline Marketing Strategies

- Jot down the offline marketing strategies you intend to apply (print advertising, direct mail, community events, referral programs).

BEST DENTAL MARKETING

OUR BEST DENTAL MARKETING IDEAS

OUR BEST DENTAL MARKETING IDEAS

OUR BEST DENTAL MARKETING IDEAS

OUR BEST DENTAL MARKETING IDEAS

BEST DENTAL MARKETING

OUR BEST DENTAL MARKETING IDEAS

OUR BEST DENTAL MARKETING IDEAS

OUR BEST DENTAL MARKETING IDEAS

OUR BEST DENTAL MARKETING IDEAS

BEST DENTAL MARKETING

OUR BEST DENTAL MARKETING IDEAS

OUR BEST DENTAL MARKETING IDEAS

OUR BEST DENTAL MARKETING IDEAS

OUR BEST DENTAL MARKETING IDEAS

OUR BEST DENTAL MARKETING IDEAS

OUR BEST DENTAL MARKETING IDEAS

OUR BEST DENTAL MARKETING IDEAS

OUR BEST DENTAL MARKETING IDEAS

OUR BEST DENTAL MARKETING IDEAS

OUR BEST DENTAL MARKETING IDEAS

ND MARKETING IDEAS

OUR BEST DENTAL MARKETING IDEAS

OUR BEST DENTAL MARKETING IDEAS

OUR BEST DENTAL MARKETING IDEAS

OUR BEST DENTAL MARKETING IDEAS

OUR BEST DENTAL MARKETING IDEAS

STAY CONNECTED AND KEEP INSPIRING

The constantly evolving landscape of digital marketing ensures that there will always be new techniques and strategies to learn and apply. Your resourcefulness and dedication to refining your craft will keep you at the forefront of this exciting industry.

For more insights, tips, and strategies, visit BestDentalMarketing.com. Our goal is to become your go-to resource for all things related to Dental Marketing. We regularly update our website with informative content that will help you stay up-to-date with the latest trends and best practices in the industry.

We also invite you to stay connected with us. Share your stories, experiences, and successes. We'd love to hear about the innovative strategies you've implemented and the milestones you've achieved. Your journey fuels our passion, and your success stories inspire us to create even better content.

We understand that creating an impactful and inspiring Dental practice is no easy feat - it requires determination, constant learning, and an unwavering commitment to your patients. So, as you continue on this journey, remember to keep your patients at the heart of all you do. It's your commitment to them that will truly set your practice apart.

Here's to your continued growth and success in transforming smiles and making an enormous impact on your patients' lives. We look forward to continuing this journey with you.

Until next time, keep smiling!

The Best Dental Marketing Team

Made in the USA
Columbia, SC
31 March 2025